Jamie Gough is an economics researcher and lives in London. **Mike Macnair** teaches law at Oxford University. Both have been involved in the gay liberation movement since the early 1970s.

Jamie Gough and Mike Macnair

Gay Liberation in the Eighties

Pluto  Press

London and Sydney

First published in 1985 by Pluto Press Limited,
The Works, 105a Torriano Avenue, London NW5 2RX
and Pluto Press Australia Limited,
PO Box 199, Leichhardt, New South Wales 2040, Australia

Copyright © Jamie Gough, Mike Macnair, 1985

Cover designed by Roy Trevelion

Phototypeset by A.K.M. Associates (U.K.) Ltd,
Ajmal House, Hayes Road, Southall, London

Printed in Great Britain by Guernsey Press, Guernsey C.I.

British Library Cataloguing in Publication Data
Gough, Jamie
    Gay liberation in the eighties.
    1. Homosexuality
    I. Title   II. Macnair, Mike
    306.7′66   HQ76.25

ISBN 0 86104 685 4

Contents

Acknowledgements

Many of the ideas in this book were initially developed in discussions with a number of comrades in the International Marxist Group. We are particularly indebted to Theresa Conway and Peter Purton with whom we have had many discussions about lesbian and gay politics over the years, and who provided invaluable criticism and suggestions when we were writing this book. We would also like to thank Bob Cant, John Fletcher, Don Milligan, Sue Owen, Bob Sutcliffe and Dave Whitfield for their help, and our editor at Pluto, Paul Crane. The manuscript was typed by The Typing Pool, London WC1.

Introduction

In 1983 the Labour controlled Greater London Council gave £¾ million to set up a lesbian and gay centre in London, run by an elected committee of lesbians and gay men. This was the first time that a British government institution had allocated a really substantial sum to meet the specific needs of gay people. The action was condemned and ridiculed by the Tory party and the press. The London *Standard* reported the views only of local people who threatened violence against the centre and the people using it. The funding of gay organisations became part of the government's justification for abolishing the GLC. When this threat was debated at the 1983 annual conference of the Trade Union Congress, the General Secretary elect of the electrician's union, Eric Hammond, said that a vote for the GLC labour group was a vote for 'terrorist groupies, lesbians and other queer people'.

These incidents illustrate how the question of lesbian and gay sexuality has become one of the issues of political debate between right and left, including the right and left within the labour movement. This would not have come about without the activity over the last fifteen years of the women's movement and gay movement, demanding that gender and sexuality should be seen for what they are – political questions. The increased prominence of issues of sexuality within the conventional forums of politics raises new questions. Women and gay men who are involved in action around issues of sexuality are asking about the connection of these issues to other political struggles; where and how do we find allies? People active on the left and in the trade unions are beginning to recognise the issues of sexuality, and to question their relation to traditional labour movement priorities. We have written this book to try to give some answer to these questions.

Underlying the problems of political activists are the concerns of 'ordinary people'. And, though less systematically, these concerns also raise the question of the relation between sex and politics. Life in Britain today is riven with tensions which run through every aspect of people's lives, from the office, factory or dole queue to the bedroom. Sexual and close emotional relationships are no less a subject of conflict and anxiety than issues traditionally considered as 'political'. Millions of people are finding that the old formulas of romance, family life and parenthood do not bring happiness; millions are trying to find ways out of the roles that have been assigned to them. The failings of the present arrangements for sexual relationships are felt all the more acutely to the extent that 'good sex' has come to be seen as a vital part of individual achievement, essential to the 'pursuit of happiness'. Where fifty years ago people might have been content if they could consider themselves 'a good mother' or 'a skilled worker', people now feel that they must also be a good lover. Yet sex seems in many ways to be more rather than less problematic than before.

Anxiety and unhappiness in sexual relationships are paralleled by increasingly sharp economic dilemmas: to demand a wage rise or not, to strike or not, to leave a lousy job or not, to move in search of work or not. But an important difference remains between economic problems and sexual problems. Most people see some connection between their own increasing financial problems and the increasingly polarised political debate over strategy for the economy. Unhappiness with sexual relationships, however, largely appears to people as an individual failing which requires individual solutions. The vast discussion of sex, whether with intimate friends, in TV soap operas, or in the sensational sex stories, sex quizzes and sex guides of the tabloids, seem to lead back to one point: you are inadequate, you must try harder.

But people are also becoming aware, in varying degrees and ways, that sex is not something purely individual or separate from other aspects of their lives. Millions of women know that their sex lives are limited or dictated by financial dependence on men. Millions of women have experienced the inadequacy of abortion facilities and know that this is a result of political choices. Millions of young people known that their sexuality has been restricted by having to live with their parents. And many people know that their sex lives have involved power relationships and that these power relationships are in some way wrong and unnecessary. The media notwithstanding, people do make these connections. The link between sex and politics, the way in which sex is political, is not just a concern of left political activists; it is already an important question for the majority.

Our aim in writing this book is to look at this link. Our immediate concern is with the problems of lesbians and gay men, who together with other groups like women and young people, are sexually oppressed in our society. But we think that, in the end, the question of lesbian and gay liberation is inseparable from the whole organisation of sex and from the lives led by heterosexuals. Indeed, we will argue that lesbian and gay liberation implies the eventual disappearance of heterosexuals – and homosexuals.

The book is written as an argument: that lesbian and gay liberation is a necessary part of making a socialist society, and that this liberation cannot come about except through this wider project. We therefore take issue with those people who see themselves as socialists but who think that defending the rights of lesbians and gay men is something of a tactical liability, or a luxury, or no more than a matter of philanthropic concern for a 'disadvantaged group'. We also want to argue that lesbians and gay men who are concerned for our rights and our liberation should organise their activity in a socialist way, and should look for allies and connections with other organisations fighting for socialism. Our argument, then, is that the connections which have started to appear between lesbian and gay politics and the socialist movement need to be developed and deepened; and we make some suggestions about how this can be done.

The theme we have chosen, and the comparative shortness of the book, mean that there are many important issues of current debate that we do not discuss, or touch on only implicitly. We do not compare other theories of sexuality with our own approach, nor do we go into the issues raised by recent re-examinations of psychoanalytic theory. We think, nevertheless, that the discussion we give is sufficient for the point we wish to make, and that these exclusions may enable us to make up in clarity what we lose in richness.

We are conscious that it is in many ways presumptuous for gay men to write a book which claims to be half about lesbian politics. A book on the same subject written by women would doubtless be very different. But we think that to write a book about gay men and socialism would be, not so much 'incorrect' for 'leaving out lesbians again', as theoretically and politically incoherent. We *do* need more discussion among gay men about our specific sexuality and political relations. But we think that it is impossible to think about, or act on, the relation between gay men's liberation and socialism in any systematic way without tying it to (and in a sense starting from) the situation of women, and of lesbians in particular. *This* book does have to be about lesbians and gay men. In taking this subject, however, we do not want to gloss over the vital differences that exist between the situation and oppression of lesbians and gay men.

In this connection there is a particular question of language. The issue of gay male sexuality has always been more prominent in public discussion and ideas than that of lesbianism, even to the extent that lesbians have been 'invisible', seen as non-existent. As a result, use of the words 'homosexual' and 'gay' tends to gloss over the specific interests and identity of lesbians. We prefer, then, to speak of lesbian and gay sexuality, and of lesbians and gay men. However, when writing a book on the subject, these phrases can make for a pretty turgid style if used constantly. We therefore sometimes use the word 'gay' or 'homosexual' to refer to both women and men. We hope that this usage will not obscure the many important differences that we discuss between the situation of lesbians and that of gay men.

1. Gay life today

A stubborn minority

Children of lesbians would suffer from having no father,
which could lead to a confusion of the child's sexual
identity.

> Director of the National Children's Bureau, 1978

The homosexual relationship breeds no such natural
corrective (children), no compulsion to be outward-looking,
and to enter, as in a family, into new and ever-growing
relationships. It is, in more ways than the obvious one,
sterile.

> Guide Association, early 1970s

The paramount reason for the introduction of this Bill is
that it may at last move our community away from being
riveted to the question of punishment of homosexuals
which has hitherto prompted us to avoid the real challenge
of preventing little boys from growing up to be adult
homosexuals. Surely, what we should be preoccupied with
is the question of how we can, if possible, reduce the
number of faulty males in the community. How can we
diminish the number of those who grow up to have men's
bodies but feminine souls.

> Leo Abse MP, House of Commons speech, 1967, on the
> Bill to liberalise the Sexual Offences Act

When we recognise ourselves as lesbian or gay, the first thing we become aware of is that there is something 'wrong' with us. And not only that: our own feelings about ourselves are 'wrong'. Society tells us that we are 'sick', that our sexual desires are 'unnatural', though they seem to come quite naturally to us. Before we even dream of gathering up the courage to act on our desires we are told that we are virtual rapists, that no member of the same sex is safe from our advances, that sex is constantly on our minds. We discover that we have a mission in life: to convert as many people as possible to 'our ways'. Indeed, our mere presence may be enough to 'corrupt' the young. Nor does our sickness limit itself to our sexuality: we learn that our whole personality is deformed. We are immature, selfish, childish. If we are lesbian we must be aggressive, insensitive, hard. If we are gay men, we must be weak, oversensitive, soft. We are the opposite of everything that is balanced and normal.

We experience these prejudices continually from the people we come into contact with every day – relatives, fellow workers, other students at school, people in the street. The rejection, derision and violence that result are things that we have to constantly deal with and which we constantly seek to avoid.

It is not only this general background of hostility that bears down on us. We find that there are countless practical barriers to our meeting with other gay people and to forming sexual relationships with them. If we are openly gay our families may turn us out. We are in danger of losing our jobs, of police harassment, and of attack by 'queer bashers' and fascists. Yet despite these enormous pressures, millions of people in Britain lead a lesbian or gay life of some kind and regard homosexuality as in no sense inferior to the heterosexual norm.

There are many starting points. Some of us have known we were 'different' since we were at school and have always lived as gay. Others – especially women – have felt forced to live as heterosexuals before being able to come out; many lesbians have enjoyed heterosexual relationships, but have then changed.

The common starting point – and one that distinguishes gay

people from all other oppressed groups – is that we first become identified as part of the gay minority by ourselves rather than by others, and thus as an isolated individual. Gay people are not born into any particular class or social group. There is no identification or collective existence as is the case with, for example, black people. From this point we then have to overcome the many barriers to living with other gay people.

The ways in which we live as gay are also enormously varied. Many people have more or less infrequent gay encounters against a background of celibacy or a long-standing heterosexual relationship or marriage. Some have a gay affair 'on the side'. Others (and this is particularly true of gay men) have frequent promiscuous gay sex. Others form gay couples; a few have more than one steady gay relationship.

Within each one of these situations, there are different ways of declaring or not declaring our 'gayness', of 'coming out'. For many gay people, gay life consists simply of not marrying. Many have sexual relationships known only to the participants. Others can confide their sexual fantasies or activities to close friends. A few declare their gayness more or less indiscriminately to the world at large. Paradoxically, this generally does not involve saying anything about sexual activity; it simply involves doing all the other things that gay people are supposed to do, and particularly acting like the opposite sex. The butch woman will be regarded and treated as a lesbian by most people; the effeminate or camp man will be regarded and treated as gay.

Every time we come out in a new situation or with new people we are taking a risk, a risk of ostracism, of rejection, or of violence. We stick our head above the parapet, knowing that there is a barrage of missiles flying overhead. It can be a terrifying experience, and it can take years of mental debate to do it; and yet we do it.

A particular way of coming out is to participate in the gay scene, by which we mean all those organisations and places where gay people go to meet and be with other gays. The scene is private in that it excludes (or attempts to exclude) heterosexuals, but public in that it goes beyond the purely private gay encounter or affair. Here we can come out more safely than elsewhere. It is a way of having a bit of gay life in an anti-gay world.

The gay scene is itself enormously varied. It includes private gay parties; gay pubs; public areas like particular parks and public toilets where gay men meet for sex; lesbian and gay social groups; groups for gay people with sporting or other interests; gay hotels and travel services; and, particularly in the big cities, clubs and discos. The larger the city, the more these social activities are divided up by different groups of gay people: between men and women, between classes, between races, between gay people (gay men in particular) with different styles and sexualities. In the smaller towns, gay people have to submerge their differences or remain isolated. The gay press, gay contact ads and the gay telephone information services provide links between this social scene and individual gay people. *Gay News*, before its closure in early 1983, had a circulation of 50,000; the London Gay Switchboard has received over a million calls within its first ten years.

In addition to social groups, there are a large number of gay organisations formed specifically for political and cultural ends. Lesbian, gay youth and gay black groups; the Campaign for Homosexual Equality and the Scottish Homosexual Rights Group; gay groups within political parties; gay trade union and professional groups; theatre, film and video groups and gay publications; counselling and befriending services: all these exist to go on the offensive against the hostile straight society.

To the extent, then, that we begin to lead a gay life of some kind we tend to become part of that alien minority, gay people. We do this, in the first place, on terms set by our oppressors. But at the same time we stop being their objects and start actively to shape our own lives.

Present day society is a problem for gay people; but also, gay people are a problem for present day society. This is our starting point in this book.

The sex police

Many of the most powerful groups and institutions in Britain systematically attack gay people and discriminate against us. We will call these groups and institutions the 'sex police'.

The law and the judges: perverted justice
> The roots of good social behaviour . . . are to be found in the home, in a stable family life . . . (But) instead of encouraging youngsters to think straight . . . (society) deliberately blurs those very boundaries which ought above all to be clearly defined . . . The men who, by today's jargon are described as gay, are not gay, they are homosexual and/or buggers and it is a pity that they are not called that. Easy and soon to become easier divorce; the pill on demand at the age of 10 . . .; legalised abortion . . . They've all made their contribution to our present condition.
>
> Lord Lane, Lord Chief Justice, 1983

The law underpins the rule of parents over their children. If gay youth leave home before they are 16, the law will return them. In deciding whether a young person is out of control of his or her parents, attempts to lead a gay lifestyle or to come out as gay are often used as criteria; they are used in decisions concerning care (a particularly arbitrary form of detention). The criminal law is sometimes used to prosecute young people. More often, it is used to persecute them – to break up their sexual relationships; and it frequently leads to the so-called 'victim' being put into care.

Contrary to what is often supposed, the taboo on adult male homosexuality is still firmly enshrined in the law. Just as the 1967 Abortion Act did not legalise abortion but merely made it allowable under certain circumstances, the 1967 Sexual Offences Act did not legalise male homosexuality but merely allows it in certain conditions. Buggery (which carries a maximum sentence of life imprisonment) and other forms of sex between men ('gross indecency') are in general *illegal*. They are permitted only between adults over 21 'in private'. It isn't 'in private' if more than two people are present, or if it's in a locked cubicle of a public toilet.

Lesbian sex has an age of consent of 16; it is also illegal in whatever the courts define as 'public' places. In practice lesbians are rarely prosecuted. But this doesn't mean they're in a better position than gay men. It reflects a desire on the part of parliament and the courts to avoid acknowledging and publicising lesbianism. Also, the general oppression of women has meant than an open lesbian subculture of significant size has only appeared recently, so that criminalisation has been considered unnecessary.

The laws on gay sex are reinforced by others which prohibit both actions designed to get gay sex and indeed many acts in public which simply have gay overtones. For a man to chat up another man (or for a woman to chat up a man for paid sex) is illegal; not so men soliciting women. Kissing and displays of affection in public by people of the same sex ('outraging public decency'); letting people have gay sex in your house ('keeping a disorderly house'); publishing gay lonely hearts ads; introducing gay men who subsequently have sex together ('procuring buggery or gross indecency') are all illegal. Having a gay party in your house and running a gay bar or disco are probably also illegal. Note that most of these offences apply equally to lesbians as to gay men. The idea that the criminal law attacks only gay men is a myth.

The judges add their pennyworth of bigotry. Several anti-gay laws have been invented by the judges ('common law'). In general the judges' view is that though gay sexual acts in private between men over 21, and between women over 16, cannot be punished, homosexuality is 'unlawful'. Accordingly, for them it is legitimate to discriminate against gay people; indeed, it is 'the policy of the law' or 'public policy' to do so. Thus, sacking gay people because of their sexuality is in general not unfair dismissal. Homosexual advances may be treated as provocations sufficient to reduce murder to manslaughter and let a killer off with a suspended sentence.

The most constant and severe victims of this judicial bias are lesbian mothers. In divorce proceedings ninety per cent of openly lesbian women lose custody of their children. Before 1976 the courts often made it a condition before granting custody that the woman would live apart from her lover or remain celibate. While this is no longer done, many lesbians are forced to lead a life which will not offend the prejudices of judges in order to ensure that they will be allowed to live with their children.

The police

The police use their wide powers of discretion under the law in ways that are anti-gay. Where crimes, such as sex in public, apply equally to heterosexual and gay sex, the police only enforce the law against gay people. A large amount of police time is devoted to patrols and raids on gay clubs and cruising areas. Police *agents provocateurs* are used to get gay men to commit crimes for which they are then prosecuted. Systematic investigations of gay male milieux are carried out using threats of prosecution, or of disclosure to family or employer, to gather information for prosecutions. Police powers to arrest on suspicion are used against gay people as they are against blacks. The police frequently reveal that someone is gay to their employer or family, knowing that this revelation may have a devastating effect on their lives.

The police are motivated by their own anti-gay prejudice, reinforced by anti-gay training manuals. Since gay 'crimes' are numerous, some are easy to detect, and many gay people plead guilty to avoid publicity. Arresting gays is also an easy way to get prosecutions, a basis for police promotion. Arrests of gay people are often made on a large scale within a short period, so that the press can give the impression of rampant vice and of effective police response.

Avowed lesbians and gay men, like other oppressed groups, are the subject of police violence. On the other hand, the police make little attempt to prevent 'queer bashing' and often show sympathy with queer bashers. It has even been suggested that 'queer bashing' can best be controlled by keeping up the level of indecency prosecutions against gay men.

Fascist groups
Hundreds of thousands of gay people fell victim to Hitler's pogroms and concentration camps. The main issue of contemporary British neo-Nazi groups – the National Front, National Party and British Movement – is racism, and their main active support comes from white working class youth who are involved in 'Paki-bashing' and 'queer bashing'. They also find support among prison and police officers. All these neo-Nazi groups support the Nazis' extermination of gay people and propagate anti-gay ideas in particularly vicious forms. They have organised 'counter-demonstrations' and violence against gay political activities and gay centres.

The medical profession and the medical bureaucracy
We consider homosexuality to be pathological, bio-social, psychosexual adaptation consequent to pervasive fears surrounding the expression of heterosexual impulses.
Irving Beiber, *Homosexuality, a Psychoanalytic Study,* 1962

From the mid-nineteenth century, the medical profession played a central role in shaping ideas about gay sex and gay people; homosexuality was no longer simply a sin and a crime, it was also a medical disorder. Since the early 1970s this idea has been on the decline in medical circles, if not outside. Nevertheless, the World Health Organisation still lists homosexuality as a mental illness, and many doctors still subscribe to the idea that gay people are mentally ill. These ideas dovetail with medical beliefs and practices towards women, which tend to treat women as naturally neurotic, unstable or infantile.

Gay people are now unlikely to be compulsorily committed to hospital by relatives – but it does still happen. Gay people convicted of trivial offences may be sent to mental hospitals by the courts. Many doctors still discriminate against gay people. Some still invite gay patients who approach them about other problems to take courses of 'treatment' for their sexuality. These treatments involve hormone implants, aversion therapy and drugs.

Within physical medicine, the specific needs of gay people are scarcely catered for at all. Lesbians in particular are discriminated against because gynaecology is completely geared towards the childbearing role of women. Internal examinations are only regularly provided through family planning clinics. If a lesbian does persuade a GP to perform this important regular check-up, she will doubtless be asked when she has had 'sexual intercourse' (meaning heterosexual penetration). There is disproportionately little research on diseases which specifically affect lesbians and gay men, compounded by lack of teaching and information on these to medical staff. To add insult to injury, it is then once again implied that there is something necessarily 'diseased' about gay sexuality: this is the theme of much that has been written by the medical profession about the current epidemic of Acquired Immune Deficiency Syndrome (AIDS).

Teachers and the Local Education Authorities

The education system does its best to ensure that young people grow up straight – and in doing so oppresses both young people growing up gay and gay teachers. Most schools regard homo-sexual activity by pupils as grounds for punishment or dismissal, and pupils who are openly gay are harassed and sometimes expelled. Teachers have been sacked even for being 'discreetly gay'. More often, teachers are simply expected to stay in the closet: John Warburton was banned from teaching by the Inner London Education Authority for refusing to promise not to respond to students' questions about his sexuality.

Many schools' timetabling and options reflect straight gender types (male carpenter, female cook), which are particularly oppressive to young women but also to those gay youth, whether male or female, who fit less easily into their gender stereotype. 'Sex education' usually ignores gay sexuality completely, or presents it as 'a phase you may go through'.

The importance attached to this aspect of sexual policing is indicated by the press witch hunt in 1978 against a lesbian feminist teacher, Sally Shave, who wrote an article on fighting sexism in the classroom.

> Parents can't help smiling fondly when they watch their daughter taking half an hour to decide which cardigan goes best with the dress she is planning to wear tomorrow. Or their small son putting on the muddy trousers he took off the night before because 'they're the comfortable ones' . . . You have only to think how worried you'd be if it was the other way round to realise what pernicious rubbish Sally Shave is talking. And to wonder why Hertfordshire education authorities allow her to practise her half-baked theories. (*Evening News*, September 1978.)

Anti-gay agitators

The press, particularly the Tory tabloids, but also the 'qualities' and the 'Labour' *Daily Mirror* keeps up a barrage of anti-gay attacks on gay people that are sometimes overt and hysterical, sometimes subtle and snide. *Daily Mirror* columnist Peter Tory wrote of tennis player Chris Evert as 'a refreshing contrast to the lesbian creatures who often dominate the Centre Court these days'.

TV soap operas, sitcoms and standup comics continue to feature anti-gay jokes, 'camp' gay men and 'butch' gay women. For the TV companies we *exist* primarily as a joke, reflecting the mixture of aggression and uneasiness that makes up anti-gay feeling. It is extremely rare for TV drama to portray gay people as we are, even rarer to present situations from our point of view. The token current affairs programme about gay people is usually just that – 'about' us, not by us; and where we do get access censorship tightly limits what can be said. The media, though the most powerful, are not the only anti-gay agitators. Alliances have been formed between hard-line conservative politicians, orthodox churchmen, and individual prurient busybodies like Lord Longford and Mary Whitehouse to promote campaigns through organisations like the National Viewers and Listeners Association, the Society for the Protection of the Unborn Child and the Care Christian Action Research and Education Trust (CCARET) (formerly the Nationwide Festival of Light). The media give far more attention to the views and actions of these organisations than comparable ones on the left.

Gay people have always been a prime target for these groups. Mary Whitehouse initiated the prosecution of *Gay News* in 1977 for 'blasphemous libel' in publishing a gay poem about Jesus. CCARET aims among its other activities to 'try to interest younger members of the protestant churches in its views on (e.g.) homosexuality'. (*Gay News*, No. 263)

Employers

Many gay people who are open about their sexuality, or who are 'found out', lose their job. Employers are particularly likely to sack a gay person in a job involving children or young people, due to the danger of 'corruption'; or in one involving contact with the public, in case offence is given. Homosexual acts between consenting adult men are still illegal in the Army, Navy, Air Force and merchant navy; lesbian sex is illegal in the armed forces. In certain departments of the civil service homosexuality may be grounds for transfer on grounds of 'security'.

Gay people are often openly driven from jobs by the prejudice and aggression of their fellow workers. Trade unions are erratic in defending sacked gays, and do virtually nothing to support gay people who come out at work or to combat prejudice among non-gay workers. So, like members of other oppressed groups, many gay people, particularly if they are working class, end up unemployed or in badly paid, temporary and transient jobs.

Property owners and financiers
The scarcity of housing and the way it is managed make it difficult to live outside the family. It is more difficult for women to get mortgages than men because their income is typically lower. It is difficult to get a joint mortgage unless you are a married couple (actual or potential). Council housing is designed and largely reserved for married couples, people with children, and the elderly. On top of this, public and private landlords and building societies sometimes discriminate against gay people as such. A quite disproportionate number of gay people therefore end up in the privately rented sector. This is the form of housing that has received by far the least state subsidy. It is the most expensive, the poorest quality, and the most insecure.

Controllers of public services
Unconventional-looking gay people, men and (especially) women, and gay people who express affection for each other publicly, are discriminated against by pubs, hotels and social clubs which are not part of the 'gay scene', and sometimes also by places with a large gay clientele. Gay organisations are constantly refused the hire of buildings for social events and conferences, by both private firms and local authorities. Councils often refuse to stock gay material in their libraries. Most newspapers will not take any gay ads. Gay publications have problems with distribution, finance and printers. Unmarried women, including lesbians, are discriminated against in many types of credit transaction.

Thus in every field of public life, gay people are liable to be oppressed and treated unequally.

Family life

Inequality and oppression, however, start at home. Gay people are told: you are bad because your sexuality prevents you from marrying. You are 'unnatural' because you do not create children, the natural function necessary for the future of society. You are 'sick' because you cannot enjoy that great pleasure – family life. You are incapable of deep relationships because you do not tie yourself within a marriage. These criticisms, felt deeply by many people, are repeated endlessly by establishment moralists. But it is not only ideas and feelings about the family that lie behind anti-gay prejudice. The very arrangements of family life are profoundly oppressive for gay people.

In the ideal modern family, Man is Father, Breadwinner and Boss; Woman is Mother, Housewife and Homemaker. They are eternally monogamous and have two or three children; the little boy plays cowboys, the little girl plays 'house', and neither of them plays with their private parts.

In the real world, if the husband goes out to work, his work is the 'real' work and he is the 'real' person. Though he may do a little washing-up from time to time, everything else is subordinate to his work. He comes home tired in the evening and has to be provided for; he wants his sexual favours; he may get violent if thwarted; he administers discipline to the kids; he is the main source of cash. He has a little power in his family. But the power of these other people, and of the impersonal forces of the market, is such that his little power at home is nearly all he has; so he clings to it.

The wife may or may not go out to work. In most working-class households her wage is essential. Moreover, many women go out to work because they feel it makes them more independent. But in the home she is still her husband's slave. At the end of the day it's down to her to do all the work that has to be done in the household; cooking, cleaning, washing, controlling the kids, keeping them clean, entertaining them and servicing her husband. 'A woman's work is never done.' But one husband will say to another: 'My wife doesn't work.'

While the kids are small, though, the wife would have a hard time of it to support herself and them without her husband. There are few nursery facilities if any, and they are pricey; the best jobs are kept for men; women are 'last in, first out'; and 'women's jobs' are much worse paid than men's.

All this tends to feel like the natural state of things. The cost or plain lack of availability of cooking, washing and child care provided outside the family makes these appear to be naturally private tasks. The husband has been brought up to expect domestic service; mother cleaned up after him and told his sisters to help out. Therefore the wife would feel bad, or wrong, or unnatural not to be servicing her husband; even if they agreed to share the housework she would notice the dirt before he did; she'd feel as if she was nagging him to do his share.

Children grow up under the power of their parents. As children, any behaviour which is obviously sexual in adult terms is repressed. But this operates in very different ways for boys and girls. Boys may be told not to play with their penis, but they are aware of its existence and are quite likely to see it as a source of pleasure. Little girls on the other hand are usually not even aware of the existence of their clitoris. 'Why haven't I got one like him?' is rarely met with the truthful answer 'You have, it's just different'. The differences are not just about attitudes to the body. Young girls are brought up, in ways which are sometimes obvious, sometimes hidden, to think that their role in life is to catch a man and then look after him. Her pleasure, including her pleasure in sex, is to be derived from making him happy. There is little idea that women can or should seek sexual pleasure for themselves. By contrast, male sexual desire is elevated into an irresistible force. As an adult, a man who sleeps with many women is a romantic figure, a Don Juan, a great stud; a woman who sleeps with many men is a slag, a whore, a nymphomaniac.

It is not surprising, then, that among adolescents conscious sexual attraction to people of the same sex is more often experienced by boys than girls. Many young women feel emotionally drawn to another girl or woman, but do not think that this has anything to do with what they are supposed to feel for their future husbands. They don't think their sexuality is perverted because it doesn't occur to them that they have one.

This is one reason why many more lesbians than gay men get involved in long running heterosexual relationships which they do not enjoy. For many women in this situation, the lack of enjoyment does not strike them as out of place.

It is, then, initially within the family that boys and girls learn, in very different ways, that they must pair off to form new families, affirming their parents' role. This process of pairing off is the basis for the vast apparatus of sexist and heterosexist culture – women compete for men, men for women, as in a market. The tough or go-getting man and the melting dependent woman are celebrated in fiction and advertising. Women must look right to get a man; men must act right to get a woman. Sexist publicity advertises not only the commodity on sale, but woman as commodity on sale: passive, sexually accessible, serving men's 'sexual needs': free, public soft core pornography.

This may seen an unrelievedly bleak picture of the family. It is certainly a one-sided one. The family is also the place in which love, affection, tenderness, solidarity, commitment, giving, physical closeness are confined. Outside is the public, impersonal world, the market-place, where we meet as strangers and competitors. To this extent the family meets human needs denied elsewhere. We find it hard to find solidarity outside, and so we look for it within a family; and this binds us into the family even when we find it painful and destructive. But the possibilities for real love and solidarity within the family can only be realised inadequately because they have to be built into relationships of power and inequality.

We can see this in the relationship of parents to their children. Most people are deprived of any real control over their work or over public affairs. Bringing up children is the one area where people can be genuinely creative. But, because children are deprived of any power or choice within the family, they are treated as products, as objects to be moulded. The creativity is strictly one way.

This is the cruel trick of the family: it seems to offer the only road to free and satisfying relationships, but in fact it operates in such a way as to make those relationships antagonistic and strife-ridden.

The family and gay people

Family life oppresses gay people in a myriad of ways. In the first place, the subordinate position of women within the family affects all society's institutions, ideas and culture. This weighs down on lesbians as it does on all women: gay men can hide their sexuality, but lesbians cannot conceal their gender.

But the oppression of women has very particular consequences for lesbians. We have already seen how the denial of active sexuality for all women is a barrier to women becoming consciously or actively lesbian. For women who do so, their oppression *as women* takes especially sharp forms. To be expected to get your man is bad enough for all young women; how much worse if you have no sexual interest in men. How much worse, if you are a lesbian, to be required to service your husband sexually. And how much worse to be economically and legally trapped in a relationship with a man when all your strong emotional and sexual ties are to women.

The lives of young gay people, female and male, are also sharply restricted by the family. Their parents have the legal right to control their lives, and can imprison them or have them imprisoned by the state to control their sexual behaviour. They are dependent on their parents for money and housing. This is the common lot of all young people under the legal age of majority and under school-leaving age. But it bears particularly heavily on gay youth because their parents are much more likely to want to restrict their sexuality than if they were heterosexual. Being compelled to live with parents severely limits the ability of all young people to find solidarity and support from others. But this is especially restricting if you are gay, since the friendship of other gay people is essential for survival in an anti-gay world.

Young people who see themselves as gay very soon realise that they are out of line with family life. They may be rejected by their parents. They certainly soon realise that they are not going to form a family themselves unless they disguise and deny their sexuality. And, in this society, this produces an overwhelming sense of being excluded. Social life in straight society is to a very large extent organised through family life and its network of relatives, and gay people find themselves on the outside of this world of closed families. Unless we are in a position to form communities or 'substitute families' of one sort or another, gay people – as individuals or as couples – can be extremely isolated.

One aspect of family relationships that is often particularly missed is having and living with children. Bringing up children is for many people the most satisfying and creative activity of their lives (for a mixture of good and bad reasons, as we have seen); and elderly people are generally forced to be heavily reliant on their children. Gay people, unless they hide their sexuality, are usually prevented from bringing up children and excluded from the pleasures and security that this can bring.

This, then, is the double bind of the family for gay people: when you're within it – as a child, or as a parent – it burns you up; when you're outside it – as an openly gay adult – it freezes you out.

Time and money

To be able to choose, to create, to be free within sexual relationships you need time and you need money. The leisure classes have always been able to afford varied living arrangements and complex sexual and emotional relationships. Most of us either have the time but no money (living on minimal welfare benefits), or some money but no time. Waged work is not organised to fit in with people's lives, but to keep increasingly expensive machinery and plants operating as much of the time as possible, and so give the greatest returns to their owners. On a full-time working week you're often exhausted at evenings and weekends. All the chores, childcare, your social life and love life have to be crammed into the narrow space between work and sleep. If you're one of the increasing numbers of shift workers, it's even worse.

For gay people time and money are particularly important. We are a minority who tend 'naturally' to be isolated from one another. We can overcome this by going to gay parties, pubs, clubs, societies, meetings, often a considerable distance from where we live. These kinds of social facilities play a much more important role in the lives of gay people than heterosexuals, but commercial facilities for gay people are often able to charge high prices because of their scarcity. If we have a lover, they are more likely than occurs in a heterosexual relationship to live at a distance. There is a particular pressure on us to move to the big city, to get a better paid job or one with social hours – not so easy to do, in the 1980s.

Gay people are dependent for our social and sexual lives on our economic position and on what the market provides, to a degree that heterosexuals are not. This is one of the reasons that gay men in particular play the role of advanced consumers in markets such as clothes, fashion and night life. Economic scarcity, then, is a further source of our oppression; and, given the enormous inequality between the pay of women and men, a particular source of disadvantage for lesbians.

Conclusion

The picture we have drawn is, of course, highly simplified. For one thing, the different strands of gay oppression that we have described interact and reinforce each other. Quite apart from the pronouncements of their leading figures, the very activities of the sex police ensure that gay life remains hidden and furtive and thus appears undesirable. The entrapment of women and of young people in the family is reinforced in innumerable ways by the criminal and civil law, and by discrimination in employment and services. Lack of money and time are major barriers to constructing any alternative to family life. And the less money and time you have, the less likely you are to be able to avoid or combat the attentions of the sex police.

From what has been said it should be obvious that there are enormous differences in the ways in which different groups of gay people are oppressed. These are sharpest between women and men; but also appear between people of different incomes, different races, different ages. It is difficult to talk about 'the typical experience of being gay in Britain'. But if there is a common experience, it is that we start as 'displaced persons': we have to try to lead our own lives in a situation where our 'nature' has already been systematically set out for us. We are the people our parents warned us against. Yet as gay people, we have been able to organise ourselves to begin to make our own lives. And the more we do this, the more we come into conflict with the sex police and with straight society itself.

2. Homosexual, heterosexual: why the division?

Why are gay people oppressed? This is really two questions: why are there gay people; and why does society oppress us? These two questions probably can't be answered separately. Early gay theorists, in the late nineteenth and early twentieth century, thought that the causes of homosexuality were biological. If that was so, these causes could be tackled separately from the causes of oppression. But since then, evidence has built up against their theories. It's now clear that the same causes, whatever they are, that make some people gay, make others anti-gay. Both gayness and anti-gay prejudice may be explained by features of the human psyche as it is formed in society.

It's common to try to discuss psychology and society apart from the physical world, apart from technology, and apart from history. We reject this approach. The physical circumstances and social relations which shape our lives and our psychology from the day we are born are produced by earlier events of the same sort: they are part of history. 'Timeless' psychology and 'timeless' sociology leave out of account the fact that the world is changing around us. So they can describe the phenomena, or point to the problem, but do not *explain* it. For example, Freud said that 'from the point of view of psychoanalysis the exclusive sexual interest felt by men for women is also a problem that needs explaining'. But the Freudian explanation of this phenomenon leads us to a social institution, the patriarchal family as it existed in Freud's day. The question why this kind of family exists can only have a historical answer.

Before embarking on our explanation for the existence and

oppression of gay people it will help to summarise our main points:

* The requirement for the survival of the human species does not mean that same-sex relationships are unnatural. On the contrary, as a species we have a capacity for these relationships. But the meaning and organisation of homosexual relations has varied enormously through history: the present arrangements are not eternal.

* The majority of known historical societies have been dominated by men and have involved the social and sexual subjugation of women. In societies with economic classes, male dominance has been organised around a particular way of caring for children, the family system. Male dominance has meant the repression of all lesbian sexual activity, and also of adult men playing a 'passive' or 'effeminate' role. Behind the repression of these types of sexual activity, then, lies the connected systems of class and family.

* Although the use of sexual capacity has actually varied enormously through history, this use has appeared as largely outside of human control: it has been 'alienated' from us. This is because sexual relationships have actually been shaped by scarcity and survival, by class and family, rather than by conscious human choice.

* In capitalist societies this alienation takes specific forms. There is a tension in these societies between the organisation of sexual activity by the family and the possibilities opened up by the market. As a result, the lack of control of our sexual capacity is experienced as sexual attraction to specific attributes of people or things, 'fetishism'. These particular kinds of attraction are then regarded as attributes of particular people. Thus 'male homosexuality' and 'lesbianism' come to be seen as particular species of sexual behaviour, and as the attributes of particular poeple, 'homosexuals' and 'lesbians'. In capitalism, then, the repression of lesbian and passive male sexual activity is transformed into the oppression of a distinct group of people, lesbians and gay men.

* The owners and controllers of wealth – the capitalist class – are committed to a system which embodies the oppression of gay people and our liberation will have to be fought for against this class. But outside of revolutionary crises, the organised persecution of gay people is carried out largely by the middle class, and does not appear as the activity of the capitalist class as such.

Is homosexual sex unnatural?

The notion of homosexuality as unnatural is connected to people's view of marriage as the 'natural' way of life. Underlying this idea is another: humans must be heterosexual and parental by nature or the species would die out. A person whose sexual activity is exclusively homosexual will (or would before the availability of artificial insemination) leave no descendants; and a society all of whose members are exclusively homosexual would die out in one generation. In this sense the Darwinian principle of 'natural selection' seems to require of us, as a species at least, to engage in heterosexual intercourse. Doesn't it therefore require a heterosexual drive? And to ensure the survival of children, does it not also require a specific attachment to our biological children, a parental instinct – or at least a maternal instinct?

These questions are important for politics. If there is a specific parental or maternal instinct, then the nuclear family, in some form, is the way of organising the upbringing of children that is most in line with our natures. If there is a heterosexual instinct, then gay people may be tolerated, but will always be freaks, scientifically sick; and we would be a minority whose position was of no particular significance to the 'normal' 'healthy' majority beyond a general humanitarian concern.

The argument for heterosexual and parental instincts has force because it recognises that human beings are animals and like all animals our species evolved by natural selection. But we are different from other animals in two particular ways. Firstly, we develop the most diverse societies at different times and places (and without significant differences in our physical characteristics developing). Secondly, as part of this, we radically transform the material world and we innovate new techniques necessary for developing our societies. Any account of what natural selection dictates to us must take account of these two points.

Natural selection requires that, at minimum, enough heterosexual penetrative intercourse has to take place, and enough children have to be brought up to adulthood, for the total population to at least remain stable. Therefore the machinery must exist in human nature to bring about these results. If it didn't humanity wouldn't be the successful species that it is.

Our first requirement, the need for sufficient heterosexual activity, does not demand a very powerful and specific 'sex drive'. There must be some factor which ensures heterosexual sex frequently enough to produce a rate of live births sufficient to compensate for the number of deaths. What this involves in something like the 'state of nature' is indicated by the fact that in hunter/gatherer societies women give birth approximately every three to four years.

There is, moreover, a constraint on the imperative to have childen. It is necessary for the present generation to survive long enough to raise their offspring. Human children are peculiarly helpless compared to other mammals, and take an unusually long time to reach physical maturity. Hence if a new child is to be brought into the world there must be enough to feed it and the existing members of society, and the time and weight load imposed by the new child must not be such as to bring the society below subsistence level. Thus the mechanism which produces children must be sufficiently flexible to ensure that they don't eat up the society that has borne them.

Our second requirement, the need for society to commit resources to rearing children up to the age of puberty, shapes us in two ways. Forms of social organisation and methods of productive activity have to allow for the time this involves. And there must be some mechanism which produces sufficient numbers of people prepared to make this commitment to children to ensure that they are in fact reared.

This is as far as the argument from natural selection alone will take us. To go further we need to add to our picture of human nature, building not on logic but on observation. The first point is that *we have a capacity for sexual pleasure which is not tied to reproductive sex*. Stimulation can come from masturbation and from many varieties of sexual relations. In many other mammals, including our closest relatives the apes, reproductive sex is governed by an 'oestrus'. Females are only capable of penetrative sex in a brief period when they are also fertile. Human women, in contrast, are continuously capable of this sort of sex; their sex lives in this respect are not governed by oestrus, nor by whether or not they are fertile. Sexual pleasure is not tied to the capacity for reproduction; in particular children get sexual pleasure from masturbation (and in some societies from sex with other people) long before puberty. This is not a product of a particular culture. It is found among all societies, however primitive and however separated; and children may be found to masturbate at very early ages, including when they have been prevented from seeing adults' sexual activities.

Moreover, as both child and adult, we have the capacity for all kinds of sexual activity not limited to orgasm, a capacity for 'sensuousness'. And not only the physical forms of sexuality, but also the things people can find erotic are much wider than reproductive sex: different activities, situations, parts of the body, things.

Our second point is that *a desire to collaborate with other people is in our nature*. *Homo sapiens* is a social animal. One fact which suggests this is the long period of infant dependence and our relative lack of natural defences. Humans can defend themselves in groups but are vulnerable alone. Another suggestive fact is that humans make the most extensive use of language of any animal. All human societies involve complex networks of social relationships extending far beyond immediate blood relatives. All this suggests that the desire to relate to other people is one of the fundamentals of human nature.

Our third point may seem even more abstract. *Commitment to the future is in our nature*. We change the world because we are thinking, planning animals who look further into the future than other animals. Conversely, when we imagine that the future holds nothing for us, we may cease to act.

In general, like other mammals, we seek pleasurable experiences and try to avoid painful or uncomfortable ones. Many of the signals of pleasure and pain are functional to our survival, the result of natural selection: eating is good for us, so it is pleasurable. Our forward-looking character modifies our response to these stimuli. We gather and hoard, and invest time and skills in tools, deferring pleasure. We cauterise wounds, set broken limbs, pull rotten teeth for the future – all, until quite recently in our history, without anaesthetic. Even more striking, in our history millions of people have sacrificed their lives in wars and civil strife for their hopes for a future in which they knew they might not participate.

We do not claim that these three aspects of our mental world are the only features of human nature. But we would argue that they are sufficient to explain the survival of the species. They can explain why human beings reproduce; it is not necessary to postulate a heterosexual drive. Sexual relations can be pleasurable in themselves, can bring us closer to others and cement our social relations. These motivations are sufficient, even if everyone was entirely 'polymorphously perverse' in sex, to produce enough heterosexual activity to meet the required fertility. Moreover, a more diffuse human sexuality is easier to reconcile with the need to limit fertility than a specifically heterosexual drive.

Our commitment to the future, coupled with our commitment to social relations, is sufficient to account for the time humans need to commit to bringing up children. Commitment to the future is a powerful force here. Most people, especially (but not only) in more primitive societies than our own, have little opportunity to invest in the long term future except in raising children.

This explanation of commitment to child rearing is more plausible than a specific commitment to one's own biological children. Primitive societies practise infanticide on a significant scale. In pre-industrial societies significant proportions of children lose one or both parents while young; yet they are brought up. In our own society, teachers and nursery nurses devote a large proportion of their lives to other people's children. Our natural, biologically determined motivation to bring up children cannot, therefore, be limited to our own biological descendants.

The three characteristics we have outlined could be enough to satisfy the natural selection requirements for human nature. It doesn't necessarily follow that there aren't any other sexual urges or parental urges written into our biology. But scientists have not found them. The variety of human social sexual regimes, which we discuss below, is powerful evidence against their existence. In addition, if patterns of sexual behaviour are strongly determined either by genes or by exposure to hormones before birth, then identical twins (who have the same genes and the same uterine environment) ought to have identical sexual orientations. This is in fact not the case. Similarly, if disposition to heterosexuality is produced by the action of hormones, we should anticipate hormonal differences between homosexual and heterosexual people. Claims to have shown such differences have been frequently made, but with monotonous regularity shown to be unsound and contradicted. Where sexual arousal in animals is a chemical/hormonal mechanism, biologists have been able to identify the mechanism. If it's there in humans, why can't it be found?

Our conclusion is that our biology and evolution give us a capacity for sexual pleasure. They give us our character as social animals that change the world, that look into the future and plan. They dictate that we have to eat and reproduce, and that we have to organise these activities socially. But this doesn't on its own dictate any particular way of organising these activities. In particular it doesn't dictate a 'heterosexual drive' or a 'parental instinct'. The capacity for homosexual relations is part of our nature.

Homosexual sex in history

Our nature endows us with a homosexual capacity but it does not define how it is used. There are records of both lesbian and male homosexual activity in a great variety of different societies: those societies without classes ('primitive societies'); the free citizens and aristocracy of Imperial China, classical Islam, ancient Greece and Rome; medieval Europe; seventeenth century England; as well as in virtually every country of the world today. This corroborates our argument for the 'natural-ness' of gay sexual capacity. But what is striking is the enormous variation in the status of gay sexuality in these societies. The status of lesbian activity was quite different to that of male homosexual activity in virtually all cases. Each was fiercely repressed in some cases, condemned but tolerated in others, and in other societies regarded as an integral part of social life. The 'natural revulsion' to gay sexuality felt by many people is anything but 'natural'.

Even more varied than the degree of 'tolerance' was the meaning and significance of lesbian and gay sexual activity. For example, in modern Britain all sexual activity between men is regarded as falling into essentially one category 'homosexuality'. Whatever the ages and classes of the men involved, and whatever sexual activities they engage in, it is equally 'homo-sexuality' (and as such, equally to be condemned). We can contrast this with Renaissance times, where male homosexual relations were lumped together with men having sex with under-age women or prostitutes under the heading 'sodomy' (and therefore equally sinful). Even more striking is the contrast with primitive societies. In these societies male homosexual behaviour is integrated in two typical ways. One is where some males are reared as females, often attributed religious or magical powers, and often married to another man. A second is where sexual relations between boys or young men and older men is part of the process of teaching skills. In these societies sexual relations between males may have meant 'magic', or it may have meant 'adulthood'. For us, it means 'taboo', 'excitement' or 'true love'. The same physical activities have a completely different significance.

Gay sexual activity has not always been the preserve of a distinct group of people – lesbians and gay men. The existence of a group of people identified as 'gay' is specific to capitalist society. This division between 'heterosexual' and 'homosexual' people connects with the modern distinction which we noted above, between 'heterosexuality' and 'homosexuality'. Gay sexual activity has in the past been seen as a universal potential, not as something embodied in particular individuals. Our present-day notion of 'a homosexual' would have been recognised in mercantile capitalist London in the eighteenth century. But in medieval Europe or ancient Greece, the notion of 'a homosexual' would simply not have been understood. The notion of 'a lesbian' or 'a gay man' with a whole set of particular inbuilt personality traits would have been even more incomprehensible. We can see then, that both the practice of homosexuality and its repression have varied enormously between different types of society. This suggests that the contemporary gay sexuality of which we drew a picture in Chapter 1 is itself not stable or eternal.

We have argued that biology gives us a specific sexual potential, but also that the practice and meaning of sex is the creation of human history. Isn't there a contradiction here? We don't think so. The human hand was developed to grasp fruits, branches, axes. It also gave us the potential to play the piano. The piano is a product of a particular human society; but it would be impossible if we did not have hands. The piano in turn has meant the development of new forms of manual dexterity. Through conscious social change we can change sexuality; but we do not do so out of thin air – we do so by developing our given sexual capacities.

Repression and male power

Although the repression of gay sexual activity has been variable throughout history, it is possible to discern a more or less constant thread. Two kinds of sexual activity have been consistently condemned and penalised: lesbian sex of any kind; and adult men who are penetrated, sexually 'passive' or otherwise 'effeminate'. The notable exceptions to this pattern are some primitive societies; ancient Sparta; and some cases sanctioned by religions. Thus certain societies (classical Athens; Imperial China; Islamic societies) approved of boys and youths acting the passive part; but not after they reached adulthood. Other societies condemn homosexual acts in theory, but tolerate pederasty in practice (ancient Rome; medieval England).

The 'natural order' offended by these tabooed practices is the system of male power and female submission, which feminists have called 'patriarchy'. Lesbian sex is women without men; and it is women actively seeking sex, not being passed passively from the hand of the father to the hand of the husband. Lesbianism implies comradeship between women, where the social order prescribes their isolation. An adult man who is penetrated or is effeminate, on the other hand, acts like a woman and thereby symbolically betrays his sex's right to power.

We do not think that male power arises from the organisation of sexual activity in any direct sense. But male power and sexuality are closely entangled. Our sexual capacity is enormously 'elastic': almost any social relationship (and indeed, almost any physical or emotional state) is capable of being erotic. But why do power relations so often have a sexual aspect? A part of the answer is that our sexual capacity implies, in the most general sense, a sexual need. The variety of forms of sexuality shows that this need is not at all specific. But the pleasure of sexual activity and the importance to us of various sexual relationships are in part based on sexual need. One aspect of this is that sexual activity derives a symbolic importance from the comforting way in which it confirms the survival and liveliness of our bodies.

This is perhaps associated with the connection of the earliest forms of our sexual pleasure – oral and anal – with the survival functions of the body.

All social relations, then, tend to have a sexual aspect. But this is particularly true of relations of power, because the conditions for sexual activity are dependent on power. At the extreme, sex is dependent on getting enough to eat. If, in order to get enough to eat, society is organised in a way that gives some people power over others, that power will be used sexually.

Male power, then, is sexual. How does the repression of women without men and of 'passive' men arise from this? The objection to them is not that they fail to do something that dominant men want them to do. (Indeed, the latter may relish lesbian sex as a 'turn-on', or may want sex with an adult man: sexual pleasure propped up on power.) The most that can be said is that they do something *different* from what the dominant man may want. Rather, the reason for the hostility to lesbianism and passive men is that *they are psychologically threatening to the rationalisations of male power*. Male power is not natural. The physical and mental abilities and needs of the sexes are much the same. Gender differences in society as it now exists are the products of up-bringing, not genetic codes.

From this perspective, patriarchy – and indeed the exclusion of any group from social decision making – appears completely irrational. In certain historical periods it may have been necessary (a point we return to below). But this kind of 'necessity' does not automatically reconcile people to their oppression. Social inequality – including the oppression of women – needs explaining. For the underdog, the reality of power might explain it; but this is very demoralising. The powerful, in contrast, must take all society's decisions, so the rationality of human beings must be concentrated in them. But even to them their power must be apparently irrational. In some way they must rationalise it.

The rationalisation of male power is contained first of all in ideas about gender roles – about the appropriate behaviour for the sexes. Independent women and effeminate men seem to throw doubt on men's prerogative of power. Its rationalisation is also contained in the rejection of lesbian and passive male homosexual behaviour: these cannot be squared with the *idea* of male sexual power, the sexual possession and domination of women by men. Lesbian sex shows that the penis is not the be-all and end-all of sexual pleasure. Passive male homosexuality shows that adult men need not derive sexual pleasure only from penetrating someone. Gender roles and the sexual taboos reinforce each other: independence in women implies lesbian sex and is therefore wrong; lesbian sex implies independent women and is therefore wrong.

We tend to believe in these rationalisations because, as long as there is no alternative to the gender system, they make it easier for *all* of us, powerful and powerless, to get along, to live our daily lives. Only when the majority cannot any longer 'get along' – only at times of social crisis and revolution – have these rationalisations been fundamentally questioned on a large scale.

The rationalisations of male power are often integrated by religion: faith is the last refuge of irrationality. In medieval and Renaissance England buggery was seen as heresy, sodomy was connected with witchcraft. They amounted to denying that male power was the only alternative, and therefore to denying the divine order. But it was male power, not 'the Judaeo-Christian tradition' or other religious traditions, that gave us the taboos on lesbian and gay sex.

The family system

Male power has economic roots. It is a part of the way society organises the production of every-day necessities and the reproduction of the species. Moreover, the way we get food, warmth, shelter, is up to the present the dominant element in our lives: it shapes and sets limits on everything else we do, including the reproduction of the species. Male power is not the result of men's and women's biology, nor of an inherent male drive to dominate. It can therefore be overthrown, as part of changing the economic system. We hope now to justify this claim.

We shall use the terms 'family' and 'class', and it may be as well to define now what we mean by these slippery words. By 'family' we mean social arrangements under which the biological parents of children are primarily responsible for feeding and housing children and for part of their socialisation up to the age of puberty. Family in this sense is a special sort of social division of labour: *societies* have to ensure that children are brought up with a family system, *parents* do the job. There is much more to the family, in different societies, than this; but this, in our view, is the bare bones on which the rest is hung.

'Class', too, is a special sort of social division of labour. To say that classes exist within society is to say three things. First, that different groups of people get incomparably different shares of the surplus produced by the society: the food, etc., left over after everyone has had enough to carry on working from day to day. Second, that different groups of people participate to completely different extents in social decision-making. Third, that the group you fall into is determined by your birth; that is to say, that most people end up in the same class that their parents were in.

A class system has existed for some thousands of years, and survives up to the present day, because it has certain strengths as a way of organising society. Most people have to work with their hands most of the time to keep us all alive, and bring up children; this has been so from primitive society up to the present. We can get more of the necessities than we need, but not enough for *all* of us to work much less. With more ingenuity and planning we could acquire more of the necessities; but if we have to do manual work most of the time, we haven't time for the planning involved. So it is advantageous to use the surplus to free people from manual work, in order to think about how to improve production and to organise it. Societies that do this will expand at the expense of those that do not. It is in this sense that we said above that a class system might be 'necessary'.

Having people live off society's surplus and letting them take social decisions involves them having power over everyone else. They will tend to consume much more than the average (so the second aspect of our definition of class leads to the first).

Specific responsibility for planning and consumption of the lion's share of the economic surplus do not by themselves produce a ruling class. These characteristics are also shared by ruling bureaucracies to which people are appointed or elected. What distinguishes a class is that its position is inherited. Thus class, unlike bureaucracy, requires a family organisation of society through which class position can be passed on from parents to children. A society in which the rearing of children was the responsibility of the community could not have classes.

So why did the family and women's oppression come into existence? Primitive human societies existed on a knife-edge: an excess of children could not be fed or raised; too few, and the society would die out. Prolonged breast-feeding, coupled with hard physical work and a limited diet, make women less likely to conceive; so children in these societies are breast-fed for up to four years. The family system translates these requirements into constraints on individuals. *You* must continue to breast-feed *your* child till it is three or four. If *you* have another child before then and food is scarce, *you* must let it die. Exclusive female responsibility for children would achieve this objective as well; but the long childhood of human beings makes this impracticable. In any event, children before they are weaned must go around with their mothers. And high mortality, both of infants and of adults, means that women must go on having children throughout the fertile period of their lives. Women must always have infants with them.

This in practice excludes women from hunting. Consequently, in primitive societies the status of women varies inversely with the proportion of meat in the diet; the more meat in the diet, the lower the status of women; until, where meat predominates, as among the Eskimos, or in cattle-herding societies, women are appropriated by men as slaves and wholly excluded from socially organised production and from social decision-making.

It seems likely that class society emerged from this type of primitive hunting or cattle-herding society. Class might be expected to come into being through the ruling class conquering the subordinate classes: 'force is the midwife of history'. At a primitive level, the technology of force is the technology of killing animals. Cattle-herding societies have private property in cattle and women; while class involves property in women and, usually, private property in the means of production. As far back as we go in history we have stories of barbarian conquerors of settled agricultural peoples becoming their rulers and their ruling classes. It is likely that the conquering peoples were more strongly male dominated than those they subjected. We can guess that this is how class society came into existence.

The oppression of women, therefore, came before (and in one sense helped to 'cause') class society. But it was not caused by human or by male 'nature' except in some very indirect sense. It was the product of the demographic and technical constraints of primitive society. Why then has it not already disappeared?

To start with, the demographic constraints are, as far as the mass of people in the world are concerned, only now disappearing. From the mid-nineteenth century in the most developed countries, infant and general mortality fell rapidly, and the incentive for many pregnancies disappeared. The twentieth century has given us more effective methods of contraception, safer methods of abortion, and bottle-feeding. These technical changes establish some of the material conditions for women's liberation.

The second reason for the persistence of the family is that it suits the ruling class for the major part of childcare to be the private and unpaid responsibility of families, and within families, of women. There is no technical reason why this should not have been a social, communal responsibility. But this would have implied a permanent shift in socially organised resources towards meeting the needs of exploited classes (as it would now).

While ruling classes have been willing to take some responsibility for childcare at certain times, it is a much more flexible and prudent policy from their point of view that this should remain essentially the private responsibility of families.

Thirdly, the family remains important to and in the class system. For a male member of the ruling class, enslaving women ensures that *his* descendants will get his property after he dies, or will get his social position. The same is true of artisans, peasants and petty traders. In the imperialist countries (the USA, Japan and Western Europe), many working class men have been able to acquire property in the form of houses, cars, furniture and so on as well. And through the family system skilled manual and non-manual workers are often able to pass on their advantage in the labour market to their children. Only the under-class of the poor, particularly those in the Third World, are truly property-less. A desire to prevent their children falling into this under-class, and the hope that they can improve their social position, is common among members of subordinate classes in capitalist society. It implies a commitment to inheritance which, in turn, implies a commitment to female monogamy. And it implies the family upbringing of children.

Fourth and simplest: the family system gives men power over women. Earlier in the chapter we discussed how sexuality is arranged around a system of male power. As a result of this, and of the apparent unchangeability of sexuality (to which we return below), men tend to find their possibility of sexual pleasure linked to their social power over women. Moreover, this power confers benefits on men in terms of housework and childcare which we outlined in Chapter 1.

Finally, the state in modern society is concerned to preserve the social order. The division between families, between men and women, between parents and children that the family system involves is a means by which it can do so: 'divide and rule' is a very ancient maxim of state-craft. This is one reason why the state maintains a series of artificial incentives to the formation and maintenance of families: tax allowances, the legal regime of marriage, and so on.

To sum up: women's oppression and male power originated in material, technical conditions in primitive society. It has continued because a number of those technical constraints have only recently been overcome, because it is functional for class society and for individuals in class society, and because men get certain benefits from it.

We can now see more precisely what kind of threat lesbian and passive male adult sex have posed to the family and the system of male power. The fact that people have practised these types of sexual activity in numerous male dominated societies shows that male power has never been absolute, that all these societies have contained rifts and tensions that have allowed the forbidden practices to take place. The greater these tensions, the greater the instability of the society, the greater the threat posed to the rationalisation of male power by the tabooed form of sex.

But this disturbance of patriarchal ideas has not in itself threatened patriarchy. The only threat to the *existence* of this system is that an alternative way is possible of controlling reproduction and organising child care, that there is no longer a need to organise economic inequality and the inheritance of private property, and that women are aware of this alternative and organise to fight for it. As we will argue, this is indeed now the situation. But it has only been so for a hundred-odd years: only recently in human history has the existence of male dominance as such been threatened.

Sex out of control

The repression of lesbian sex and of men playing the 'passive' role are, then, based on male power and the family system. To a large extent, this does not appear to us the artificial social arrangement that it is. For many people these taboos are felt to flow out of their own sexuality; and this sexuality feels like a natural force, something we are born with. Many women, perhaps the majority, cannot even imagine being sexually attracted to other women. The idea may be repulsive; or more likely, sex without a man would seem to be a non-event (as well as a socially impossible event). Most adult men are repelled by the idea of being fucked. Why does our sexuality seem beyond our control in this way?

The other side of feeling 'I could not be attracted to *that*' is the fixing of our sexual desire on particular classes of people or aspects of people. We feel: I want to have sex with X because s/he is young, cool, beautiful, has big breasts, is well hung... Or more simply: I want to have sex with X because he's a man or because she's a woman. In other words, we fasten on a particular aspect of the person, and we are attracted to *that*.

We can call this a type of 'fetishism'. Just as the superstitious imagine that an inanimate object, a fetish, has power, so we attribute the power to attract us sexually to things, to abstracted aspects of people. And this is how our sexuality seems to be beyond our control. We usually speak of fetishistic sexuality as being the attraction to particular inanimate things (leather, rubber, etc.), or to 'unusual' parts of the body (feet, for example). But this is no different in kind to the more 'normal' particularised sexuality that we all share.

It is true that we are not necessarily attracted to everyone who conforms to one of our fetishes. For many people, it is necessary to like and trust someone to be attracted to them. If this is particularly true of women it may be due to their vulnerability in a male dominated society, and be an expression of the real interdependence of people in sexual relations that men can ignore only through relying on their power as a sex. Nevertheless, fetishes of various kinds limit almost everyone's sexual desire.

An important aspect of this fetishism in modern society is that parts of our sexuality which are not fetishistic are not generally recognised as sexual. Physical tenderness and play between adults and children, for example, is done for its own sake, rather than towards satisfying some inner compulsion. Here, we are using our sexual capacities very directly, and relating to each other very directly. Because this is not fetishistic, it is not usually thought of as sexual. In a similar way, physical signs of affection between women are usually not understood to be sexual.

All fetishism involves a handing over of our own powers to some external object or agency: it involves 'alienating' our powers. Sexual fetishism involves the alienation of our sexual capacity: we do not seem to control it; rather, it seems to control us. Why is this?

We suggest that *our sexual capacity is alienated because it is exercised for alien social ends*. Sexual relations are not controlled by people for themselves, seeking to fully realise their capacities. Rather, they are regulated by a number of social institutions over which the individual has little or no control.

In the first place there are the constraints on heterosexual activity imposed by women's fertility and considerations of population growth. Secondly, the family limits sexual relations in a variety of ways. Most obvious is the appropriation of the wife's capacity by her husband. There is also frequently forcible appropriation of a daughter's sexual capacity by her father in incest (in fact, and even more widely, in fantasy). The incest taboo prevents overtly sexual relations between siblings, and between the mother and her children, at any rate beyond their infancy. Parental control of children and parental disposal of children, too, constrain more or less sharply the sexual capacity of children and adolescents. In sex relations between adults and adolescents it is the violation of parental power that is considered truly outrageous by modern society. In these ways, parents' commitment to family upbringing of the children – the product of past sexual relations – constrains present sexual relations. And, as we have seen, the power of men over women involved in the family has ideological repercussions which are obstacles to certain forms of sexual expression.

Beyond the family, the relationships of class and authority also constrain sexual relationships. Sexual relations that follow the lines of authority may pass unremarked: a man who fucks his servants, male or female, an older man who fucks a younger man or woman. But there will be condemnation where the roles are reversed, or where sex brings the low-born into high places.

But it is not simply that these social structures *limit* the development of our sexual capacities. Particularly in modern capitalist societies, sex, as a symbol, actually becomes part of the way in which these social relationships are maintained. Marriages are held together by an 'improved sex life'. A man will exert his power over others by getting them to fancy him or by fucking them. This is an ironic form of the alienation of sexual capacity. Even as it is being put to use for pleasure, it is reinforcing the opposite of pleasure – domination.

People's sexual capacities, then, are really constrained and developed by the forms of society in which we live. It is this that makes them alienated from us. The constraints of the family are particularly important because it is in the family that our earliest and hence in some ways most formative experiences take place. The first social difference that the infant encounters is a gender difference – the difference between the roles of women and men in caring for it; this is one important reason why our sexuality is organised primarily around gender. Our family upbringing – and its peculiarities – have a deep influence on our adult sexuality. The persistence of what we learn while young and its semi-conscious character gives this sexuality the appearance of being 'something I've always known about myself'. We are not, though, in an absolute sense the creatures of upbringing. The imprint of our early experiences is reinforced or contradicted by our adult life.

Our sexual *activity* may be dictated by social power, and our sexual capacity thus become alienated. But does sexual *desire* really mould itself so closely, so 'obediently', to the social roles and activities that society prescribes for us? Surely we have fantasies which are not in any direct way the product of our experiences? It is true that our desires are much more loose, more far ranging than our behaviour. But the raw material of our imagination is still the practices that occur in our society – whether in our direct experience or not. It is above all through these practices that we understand our relation to other people, and thus build our sexual desires. Desire is freer, and is in a constant state of tension with our activity. But it is not ultimately outside of society and social power.

The alienation of our sexual capacity has existed in all societies to date, but in very different forms. In pre-industrial societies it does not, for most people, create sexual fetishism. In these societies the power relationships are mostly transparent. The slave or serf's sexual capacity is the property of her owner or lord, the wife's the right of her husband, the daughter's of her father. The male power principle is here made sense of, not by fetishised sexuality, but by religion. It is true that men, and particularly high class men, can to some extent choose sex partners, and this degree of choice creates sexual fetishism of particular female or youthful attributes, standards of beauty. But the main marriageable qualities in women are wealth, strength and childbearing capacity, not 'sexual attractiveness'. We will see shortly that in capitalist societies things become very different.

Why are there lesbians and gay men?

A particular form of the fetishisation of sexual capacity is the existence of heterosexuals and homosexuals, whose sexual desire is seen by themselves and others as limited to people of a particular sex. We have seen that these individual 'sexual identities' are specific to capitalist societies. Why is this?

The family plays a crucial part in the regulation of sexuality in all class societies. But within capitalist society, the development of the economy increasingly strips the working class family of its reasons for existence. (In this section, for brevity, we will not discuss the family or the sexuality of the ruling class.) The working class family is eroded and in some cases actually smashed up by the market. A tremendous tension is set up between the family and the market and the two systems of sexuality that they involve. We will argue that the heterosexual, lesbian and gay male identities are a product of this tension.

But first, what do we mean by the 'erosion' of the family by the market? As capitalist society has developed, the tasks involved in regulating the number of children, in child rearing and in 'housework', previously the responsibility of the family, increasingly come to be performed outside the home: they are either purchased on the market or obtained as a service from the state. An early example of this was wet nursing: from the beginning of the period of manufacture – the late seventeenth century in England – and throughout the industrial revolution, women were paid to breast-feed infants not their own. The post-Second World War period has replaced this by bottle feeding. From the late nineteenth century schools have performed an increasing part of the education of children. Marketed products have also played an increasing role – toys, books, now home computers. During the twentieth century, fertility has become regulated by more effective contraception and safe abortion techniques, available on the market or provided by the state.

Other 'household' tasks have been removed from the household. The making of clothes and the growing of food have been almost totally removed. Caring for the sick, the preparation of food, the washing of clothes have been partly removed. Other tasks have been lightened by domestic appliances and new chemicals – though these have also had the effect of locating more of the work in the home: the laundry and launderette replaced by the family washing machine.

The work removed from the household in these ways is now performed by paid labour within firms or the state. It thus becomes part of what is conventionally accounted as 'the economy', the labour time that is measured and organised by society, rather than the hidden, uncounted hours of work performed by women within the home. We may say that this work has ceased to be private and become 'socialised'.

Another way in which capitalism tends to erode the working class family is through its thirst for new sources of labour. For this reason, capitalism has abolished the legal right of the husband to determine whether his wife works outside the home. By creating new and far-flung employment opportunities for young people it cuts down the power of parents to determine whether, when and whom their children will marry. For some parts of the working class this has taken extreme forms. In the industrial revolution in England, female and child labour, and high mobility of labour tended to break up family organisation. Individual factory owners themselves organised important 'family functions' by providing tied housing and the 'truck' system of payment in goods, not money. The unemployed were sex-segregated in workhouses and deported from parish to parish. Marx and Engels in the *Communist Manifesto* commented that:

> The bourgeous clap-trap about the family and education, about the hallowed co-relation between parent and child, becomes all the more disgusting the more, by the action of Modern Industry, all family ties among the proletarians are torn asunder, and their children transformed into simple articles of commerce and instruments of labour.

Further steps in this direction were taken by factory owners in the northern states of the USA in the 1830s and 1840s who accommodated their 'hands' in barracks segregated by sex, and provided meals as part of wages.

Nor were these practices nineteenth-century aberrations. The South African apartheid system enforces separation of black men and women, making marriage and the family household meaningless. Migrant workers in Germany, France and Switzerland have been similarly housed in barracks and hostels, and separated from their families for long periods. In the search for cheap labour, employers and governments in Britain have happily torn apart families of black people. As long as the supply of labour is by some means assured, the individual business pursuing its economic interests is unconcerned whether the family exists or not.

A further aspect of the erosion of the family is that the market affords scope for sex outside the regulation of the family. Before the end of the seventeenth century people who did not form their own family households still lived in other family households, as servants, apprentices, lodgers. The rise of the market has included the growth of a market in accommodation, food, etc.; and the growth of urban, industrial, impersonal employment. This makes it possible to live – at least in the big cities, and this century in most towns – wholly outside the family, and therefore outside of the intimacy and social control involved in family life. That this implied more sex outside the family can be seen from the appearance of the gay scene in early eighteenth-century London and in the steady rise of illegitimacy figures in the same period (the latter reaching a peak during the dislocation of the family during the industrial revolution). These trends have continued this century and particularly in the last twenty years.

Finally, over the last hundred years or so, the tensions surrounding the family have allowed women to form a movement for their liberation, and this has further prised open the jaws of the family.

These developments have not, of course, abolished the working class family. The family still organises inheritance for all but the poorest; and much childcare and 'housework' is still done within it. And during the twentieth century, leisure has become increasingly home and family based. The market has replaced collective facilities – the theatre, the cinema, the pub, the football match – with private ones – radio, TV, video, computer games.

Moreover, capitalism always acts in an uneven way: it radically erodes the family in some periods, reconstitutes it in others; it builds the family of one part of the world working class while it destroys it in another. The consequence is a continuous tension between the direct operation of capital and the market on the one hand and the family system on the other.

A result of this tension is that *people increasingly enter into sexual relations with each other as 'free' individuals*. By 'free' here we mean free of arranged marriages, of parental direction, of control by the church, of legal restriction, even free from 'conjugal duty'. 'Free' also in the sense of economically independent from a father or a husband. Of course this freedom is still massively circumscribed by the family, especially for women and youth. And it is purely individualistic freedom – an absence of constraint, not a freedom to collaborate with others. In short, it is typical capitalist freedom.

The freedom to choose sexual partners has significantly increased for men during the development of capitalist society, but has increased massively for women. More choice for women means that they lose subjection to their fathers and husbands – but tend to 'gain' subjection to the male sex as a whole (just as the end of serfdom meant freedom from your particular lord but subjection to the capitalist class as a whole). You don't have to marry Smith – but you've still got to marry someone.

The importance of sex to us has meant that the space opened up by these new freedoms has been used. And indeed, sex seems to have acquired an additional symbolic importance in our individualistic society. It has become a token of our individual control of our bodies, and of the limits of that control. In sex we assert our individuality but also lose control of our bodies to ourselves or to another – a contradiction which entices us. The result has been the increasing sexualisation of our society.

The increase in freedom to choose sexual partners has been most obvious in sex outside the family, both heterosexual and gay, and in the way in which people enter into marriages. But it has also entered into the family itself. The removal of the link between heterosexual activity and child bearing, and the reduction in the total length and intensity of the (paid and unpaid) working week, allows sex more space within marriage; it particularly allows women more sexual freedom. Thus marriage, too, has become sexualised. During this century this has been evident in the rise of sexual marriage counselling, the sales of sex manuals, and the growth of 'sexual incompatibility' as grounds for divorce. This at the same time cements and destabilises the family.

More choice in a situation where there is still massive constraint, massive alienation, means more fetishism. Women's sexual capacity becomes more sharply fetishised by men. And, as women come to choose among men, male attributes too begin to be fetishised. In a market society people's capacity to produce appears to others in the form of commodities that they sell, of objects. In an analogous way, in a capitalist society people's sexual capacity increasingly appears to others as fetishised attributes.

With the increasing sexualisation of marriage, and the growth of 'markets' for lesbian and gay sex, the most important fetish becomes the *gender* of the sexual partner. The main division is then between heterosexual activity of whatever kind and homosexual activity of whatever kind, between 'heterosexuality' and 'homosexuality'. A sharp distinction is no longer made between passive adult male homosexual behaviour and other male homosexual activity: male 'homosexuality' as such is now repressed. And, increasingly, lesbian and male homosexual behaviour is put into the same category, 'homosexuality' – although lesbianism and male homosexuality in reality must remain distinct while women are oppressed as a sex.

But that is not all. Capitalist society not only makes us freer to choose our sexual partner, but the object of our desire is freer to meet our fantasy, to fit in with our fetish. *I* am attracted only to men; *you* become the type of person who responds only to men. Thus we come increasingly to be *carriers* of particular fetishised sexualities: this sexuality is both what we desire, and what we want others to desire in us. We acquire a 'sexual identity'.

Each sexual identity develops in relation to the others. The more the heterosexual identity has developed, the more our capacity for homosexual relations and other forms of sexual pleasure show up as separate categories of people: *non*-heterosexual people, people who can't or won't perform. Thus we become a heterosexual, a lesbian, or a gay man.

We can see this in the process of entering into marriage. In peasant societies the man selects the woman on the basis of her strength, her ability to work. In our society, marriages are increasingly contracted not just on the basis of sexual attraction but precisely on the basis of each partner's 'heterosexual nature'. As the productive rationale of marriage declines, this reason attains more prominence. Formerly, the obscurity of the real reasons for the formation of marriage meant that it appeared as a religious duty. Now the (ever increasing) obscurity of the reasons for marriage mean that it appears as a sexual arrangement, through a fetishised heterosexual identity.

The appearance of sexual identity is thus neither simply a product of capitalist freedom, nor simply a product of the restriction of sexual capacity by capitalism: it results from their uneasy combination. It is not a product simply of the market, nor of the family, but of the tension between them.

This complicated relationship can be seen in the history of the homosexual identity. The periods of capitalism when the homosexual identity has become sharper have not been those when family morality was waning but those when the family – and thus the heterosexual identity – has been strengthened. The gay man first appeared in early eighteenth century London. This was during the boom of family-based artisan production, family production freed from the land. The age of marriage was falling and child spacing decreasing. The gay male identity was further sharpened, and the lesbian began to appear, in the late nineteenth century. At this time the working class family was being reconstituted from its shake-up during the industrial revolution. Child labour ended, women were driven out of factory work, the male 'family wage' made its appearance, and contraception began to be widely used.

The third 'quantum jump' was during the early part of the post-Second World War boom. This was the age of family consumerism, the 'affluent society', but before the boom itself had started to erode the family once more. It is no coincidence that the Cold War ideology of the time focused so insistently on homosexuals as 'security risks'. The converse of this is that during the industrial revolution, when the working class family was radically weakened, distinctions between heterosexual and gay sex appeared less prominent. This was the era of the Napoleonic code, which took an extremely liberal line on sexual deviation.

The natures of heterosexual and homosexual identities have also changed in connected ways. From the eighteenth century up to the late nineteenth century the male heterosexual and the male homosexual were as much categories of gender as of sexuality. The eighteenth century 'molly' or the nineteenth century 'invert' was above all effeminate. To the extent that he was identified by his sexuality, this sexuality was that of the traditional taboo – *passive adult* homosexuality; and this was seen first and foremost as an outrage to masculinity. But during the twentieth century, and especially since the Second World War, the male homosexual, and increasingly the lesbian too, have more and more been defined by our sexuality, just as marriage has become increasingly sexualised. We are now as much an outrage to 'natural sexuality' as to gender roles.

We thus arrive at the greatest paradox. Within capitalism our sexual capacity, by its very nature social, has been thoroughly individualised and fetishised. Capitalism has freed our sexual capacity more than any society before it. Yet in doing so it has alienated it from us more thoroughly than ever before. This paradox is what now makes it possible – and necessary – for sexuality to be a political issue.

Fetishism and male and female sexuality

On the sexologists' findings, lesbians have fewer sex partners than gay men and are more likely to form stable monogamous relationships. There are no lesbian 'cottages' and no lesbian prostitutes. On the Kinsey findings, this difference is also the case among heterosexuals. Sadomasochism and fetishism (in the narrow sexual sense) are far less frequent among women than among men. Many women have become lesbians after seeing themselves as heterosexual for a long period, while this is much rarer in the case of men. And many women have done this through political radicalisation and involvement in the women's movement.

These are some of the differences between male and female sexuality in modern society. The right has used these differences to argue that women are naturally monogamous and so on, while some on the left have used them to argue that fetishistic sexuality is a male characteristic by which women are relatively unaffected. Either of these arguments has important strategic consequences for gay liberation and women's liberation. The first is an argument for the marriage system. The second sees instances of fetishism in women's sexuality as being due to the influence of men or capitulation to male norms. An example of this view is the equation made by some women of the Greenham peace camp between femaleness, motherhood and pacifism. Both arguments assume that the predominant features of women's sexuality in present-day society are relatively natural. We disagree with this view.

It is in one sense true that women are less likely to fetishise sexual capacity than men. This is because women have less freedom of choice than men. Within the family women are oppressed. Outside of it they are oppressed, by male-supremacist culture, by discrimination in employment, by the constant all pervasive threat of male violence and rape of women on their own. Women's sexual capacity is no less alienated than men's; if anything, it is more so. But this lack of freedom also means that we cannot infer some 'natural' female sexuality from that in present day society.

Women are not wholly unfree. And as free and yet not free, women are affected by fetishism in its broad sense. The mystique of motherhood surely combines the real social value of commitment to children with a fetishism of their childlike characteristics, as well as a fetishism of woman's reproductive capacity.

Moreover, outside the family and in the process of formation of families there does exist quite a specific female heterosexuality, a fetishism of certain male gender attributes. This is the sexuality that finds its expression in teenage women's magazines, in male pin-ups and in occasional 'what women fancy' features in the popular press.

Finally, we cannot simply equate sexual desire with sexual behaviour. For women as for men, fantasies are in general more fetishistic than their behaviour; in particular, the lesbian identity is stronger as a desire than as a practice. The gap between fantasy and action is probably greater for women than for men: while the development of the market and capitalistic freedom allows many women to imagine sexual choice, practical restrictions arising from their oppression prevent them from acting on these choices.

The positions of women and men in our society are different. Sexuality is a social phenomenon, and therefore is likely to differ as between men and women. We cannot deduce from these differences either that female heterosexual monogamy is natural, or that women are unaffected by the fetishism of sexual capacity.

Sex police and capitalists

The tension within capitalism that we have described between the market and the family is also a tension *for* the capitalist class. Individual capitalists, as employers and as sellers of commodities, have scant regard for the working class family. To this extent, they do not bother themselves about sexual morals. But, as we have seen, it is essential to all capitalists that the family is maintained. To this extent the capitalist class, particularly through its dominance of the state, will consciously promote heterosexuality and seek to suppress homosexuality.

One way in which this contradiction appears is as a difference in attitude of different parts of the capitalist class and its agents. Business which operates on an international level – and this includes a particularly large part of British capital – is so mobile and so diversified that it does not have to worry too much about the social behaviour of the working class. Or rather, it is only worried when the working class actually threatens the state. In these cases big business may become interested in sexual politics as a divisive issue: the backing of fascist movements by big capitalists in Italy and Germany in the 1920s and 1930s is an example.

It is different for medium and small businesses. They are tied to a particular workforce. The discipline of this workforce is crucially dependent on its family ties and family discipline. Its health may depend on its degree of family organisation. The middle class, too, is often threatened by the erosion of the family. Judges and magistrates, army officers, foremen and managers: all of these have jobs which involve maintaining the discipline of the population. Many teachers and social workers also see this as their main role. To these professionals, material threats to the social order and threats to their ideology are all one.

These groups, then, are constantly concerned to defend the sanctity of the family and inheritance, the immutable truths of religion and social inequality. As deferential to superior wealth as they wish their inferiors to be deferential to them, they will not attack the big capital except occasionally and rhetorically. Their fire is concentrated on foreigners and social groups that can be presented as alien minorities: Catholics, Jews, atheists, republicans, communists, feminists, blacks, Irish and particularly sexual deviants such as homosexuals. They create organisations for their purpose: the Societies for the Reformation of Manners in the early eighteenth century, the Society for the Suppression of Vice in the nineteenth century, the Public Morality Council in the first part of this century, the Festival of Light today. They agitate for tougher laws and for tougher enforcement of those that already exist. They are the principal agencies of the conscious and organised repression of gay people.

Why gay people are oppressed

At the start of this chapter we pointed out that there are really two questions involved: why are there gay people? and, why are we oppressed? Attempts to give a biological answer to both questions don't work. We have sexual capacity and human needs which are given by biology, but which don't in themselves imply any preference for heterosexual over homosexual behaviour.

The family system and the oppression of women in society explain social disapproval of adult men allowing themselves to be penetrated and of lesbian sex. Sex has become an expression of male power. These and other sexual arrangements appear to us as natural, uncontrollable forces. But behind them lies class power.

The development of the capitalist market tends to break up the social relations of the family, to integrate its material functions into the market, and to 'sexualise' it. In consequence human sexual capacities become fetishised into specific, individual sexuality. Society becomes 'heterosexualised' and throws up a layer of 'sex perverts', particularly homosexuals, who for whatever reason can't or won't fit into the social sexual norm. The development of the market place permits us to form our own social groups and subcultures and our own political movements.

But capitalism also throws up, in the smaller bourgeoisie and the middle class, a layer of people committed to the defence of the social order, the family and authority. These people, through the state or through autonomous organisations, campaign against and persecute gay people. Both the existence of gay people and our oppression, then, have their origin in capitalist society.

Can socialism get rid of the oppression of gay people? Why should socialists think it important to do so?

3. Beyond heterosexuality

Is the tension between the family system and various types of freedom created by capitalist society inevitable and permanent? Is the human capacity for sexual relations with members of our own sex doomed to be the prerogative of a minority? And are these sexual relations always going to be seen as exceptional, beside the normality of family life? If so, the greatest progress that can be achieved is a degree of tolerance for this minority, and the constructon of the best defended and most comfortable ghetto.

This cautious scenario is really a mirage. The tension we have referred to is not constant: it becomes more and more intense as capitalism develops. It is more intense in this century than in the last; it is more intense now than in the 1930s. The tension shows itself in all sorts of ways. One is the overt decay of the family system. Only 31% of households in Britain now consist of a woman, a man and children. More and more people are *forced* to live in ways to which family stereotypes give no guide. Ways of caring for people that replace the family, such as schools, the health service and social care of the elderly, are now not regarded as exceptional but as essential, 'natural'. Accompanying this has been the enormous expansion of the market and market-like freedom for heterosexuality: of heterosexual activity outside marriage, of singles bars, and – more nakedly on men's terms – of pornography and of sexual harassment.

This does not mean that the family is about to disappear of its own accord: we have seen reasons why it cannot. And people's aspirations are still strongly tied to the family. The divorce rate has increased massively since the Second World War, but so has the remarriage rate. The necessity for housework has been whittled away, yet the amount of time women spend on it has not declined substantially. As a system, the family is not disintegrating but it is becoming increasingly and painfully strained.

Another sign of the increasing tension is that, over the last forty years, the number of openly gay people and the size of the gay scene have increased continually. It is estimated that over a quarter of the population of San Fransisco is gay. And since the early 1970s, a period when stagnation of incomes has militated against the expansion of the scene, it has actually had its fastest rate of growth. Our lives become increasingly sexualised: both gay and non-gay people expect and seek 'better sex lives'; yet the strains on the family and the repression of gay sexuality, as well as the shortage of time and money, ensure frustration.

The depth of this crisis is shown by the fact that, at the same time as the gay and heterosexual identities are expanding and intensifying, an increasing number of people are consciously refusing to define themselves as either gay or straight. The most prominent examples of this to date are within the women's movement and among punk youth. These people – admittedly still a small minority – consciously reject the family and seek a sexual freedom that is not imbued with the categories that the family gives us.

What lies behind these tensions is the increasing obsolescence of the family. We have seen how capitalism itself has 'socialised' many of the tasks of the family. In the most developed capitalist countries, there is now no technical barrier to all the tasks of childcare and housework becoming the responsibility of the community. These tasks have been lightened by modern technology; and, more importantly, the time needed to produce all the other necessary goods we use has been greatly reduced. Good quality childcare, and food, washing and mending, could be provided collectively for everyone without a massive lengthening of the paid working day. It is no longer necessary for these to be inadequately provided for many people, nor for the performance of 'housework' to be ensured by imposing an unpaid second shift on women.

Because the family is obsolete, the need for it is reduced to its role in perpetuating class society. But class is itself technically obsolescent. We have seen that the technical need for a class society arises from the existence of a surplus product which is only big enough to give a minority the time to engage in social planning and decision making. But present technology, if applied to the task, could give everyone that time. The threat of the new technology is millions on the dole. But its potential is the fifteen or ten hour week. Why give decision making over to a special class, when everyone could have time to study, discuss and have access to informaton for decision making? And if we don't need a class system, why do we need the family system which ensures the inheritance of class position?

The technical obsolescence of both family and class means that there is a real basis for getting rid of them. And this real possibility has given rise, since the late nineteenth century, to mass movements to change the gender system – the women's and gay movements. It also underlies the current turmoil of sexuality. We argued above that historically the repression of lesbian and passive adult male sexuality behaviour arose from people trying to make sense of male power. These sexual activities did not constitute a material threat to male power, but a powerful threat to its rationalisations. In general, the same point can be made about the repression of lesbians and gay men within capitalist society.

But with the obsolescence of family and class, the threat posed by gay sex becomes far more potent. It is not that gay sexual acitivity makes heterosexual activity impossible, any more than it did before. But the extent of the gay scene and the number of people living as gay is *a sign that the family system is obsolescent*. Gay sexual activity will not overthrow the family system. But the family's obsolescence means that it can be superseded, and the growth of open gay sexuality is an advertisement that this is so. That this growth mainly takes the form of an increase in the number of gay people means that, to some extent, the 'problem' is insulated from the heterosexual world, is ghettoised. But it also makes the advertisement that much more striking: there are an increasing number of people whose 'nature' tends to prevent them from making new families.

This is the nature of the 'threat to the system' now posed by gay sexuality. The promise, which is the other side of this 'threat', is that gay sexual activity does not have to be walled in by the family: it could come out of the ghetto.

Socialism and the family

There is, then, a promise, a real possibility, contained in present day society. But what has socialism to do with this promise?

The classical definition of socialism is a system of common ownership of the means of production; and distribution of goods and services according to the principle 'from each according to their ability, to each according to their need'. Marxism has also distinguished three phases of socialist development. First, the 'dictatorship of the proletariat', a state geared to defend the interest of working people against reaction. Secondly, 'socialism' in the sense we will discuss it here. Third, a true economy of abundance, in which the only limits on activity are the limits of the natural world. The latter is really only a speculative possibility which may prove materially impossible. Our ideas about fighting for socialism today concern the first phase, the way in which working people can assert their collective strength. But this only makes sense as a way of moving towards socialism, so these ideas must be shaped by the strategic goal of socialism.

'The means of production' are everything we use to produce things, including the production of ourselves. They include, at the present time, factories and lathes, offices and typewriters; but also schools and hospitals, and houses, washing machines and nappy sterilisers. These are all, and equally, necessary to produce ourselves and our society. But these objects can only be produced with the application of our power to work. This labour power and the skills it involves are also part of the means of production. In present day society, labour power is bought for part of the week by employers and used according to their private plans.

The importance of 'ownership' is not its legal form but the ability to control the use of the thing which is owned. So 'common ownership' means much more than simply declaring that something legally belongs to 'the public' or 'the workers'. 'Common ownership of the means of production' means that all members of society, together, control the whole process of production.

This has two vital – and controversial – implications. The first is that without self-management and participatory democracy 'common ownership' is just a legal fiction, because without these things people cannot really control production.

The second implication is that it means a collective responsibility not just for the production of goods and services but also for all the tasks presently organised privately within the family. This is not to say that all this work should be carried on collectively. There is no reason for able bodied people not to make their own beds, for example. The point is rather that the direct production of people, as well as the production of things, becomes a collective *responsibility*; within this, it can be decided what is the most efficient and most egalitarian way of carrying out each task, what produces the best 'service' for the least effort. The labour power which is used in carrying out *all* social tasks – including collectively organised care of dependent people – is also therefore in 'common ownership', that is, its use is planned and material facilities allocated to it by society as a whole.

'The common ownership of the means of production' is, then, incompatible with the family system. It is incompatible with private responsibility for 'housework' and the care of dependents. It is also incompatible with the system of inheritance organised by the family. This is most obviously the case with the private inheritance (and therefore control) of productive facilities. But it is also true of the inheritance of skill, the passing on of skills through the family. This limits the access to these skills by all members of society. It prevents these skills, a part of the means of production, from being socially used and socially developed.

In the twentieth century, the growth of family consumption and family 'leisure' has meant that an increasingly important part of inheritance for working people has been the inheritance of lifestyle and of 'life skills'. Parents want their children to inherit and 'improve on' their lifestyle – their *family* lifestyle. As we have seen, the formation of families now takes place in a large part through the couple's heterosexual identities. Parents are thus concerned that their children should grow up straight (even when they are quite 'liberal' about other people's children). The strengthening of the heterosexual and homosexual identities has therefore been accompanied by an increasing worry about 'corruption of youth'. The modern family organises the inheritance, not only of property and work skills, but of heterosexuality itself. Family inheritance is in this sense directly anti-gay.

We can already conclude: the family is not only unnecessary to socialism, as traditionally understood; it is incompatible with it.

Divided and ruled

The family is also deeply divisive. And the divisions it creates go hand in hand with oppressive relationships and oppressive needs. This is a further reason why the family system is a barrier to making socialism.

The family divides household from household. The family household is popular with governments, civil servants and employers partly because it helps them to 'divide and rule' the vast majority of the population. One of the things that makes people unwilling to take collective strike action is the private responsibility they have for themselves and their dependents. Partly because family organisation means massive duplication of work, the family absorbs a disproportionate amount of energy and private worry. This cuts down the time people spend together, so that the problems of social life are more difficult to solve. This is a particularly acute problem for women because of their role in the home: the family divides women from women. This fragmentation makes it very difficult for working people to collaborate to pursue their interests. It would make it impossible to achieve the collaboration and solidarity needed for running a socialist society.

The work and worry of the family fall disproportionately on women. Men can escape and form social groupings at the expense of their household slaves. The organisations of the labour movement were largely built at the expense of women in the house, providing the work that freed men to go to meetings, picket lines, demonstrations. Thus the family divides men from women, half of society from the other half.

Society does, then, allow some solidarity between working class men (and very close solidarity between ruling class men). But this solidarity satisfies the human need for collaborative social relations in only a very distorted way. It is not solidarity to meet each others' needs. Fear of homosexuality sharply limits the forms of affection between men. Nor is the solidarity of men against the outside world always directed against their oppressors. It is often solidarity against women, against lesbians and gay men, and of white men against blacks.

The antagonism between heterosexuals and gay people is, as we have seen, another product of the family. It serves in its turn to sharpen up the heterosexual identity, particularly of men: men establish their heterosexuality, to others and to themselves, by abusing 'queers'. What else is heterosexuality but non-homosexuality?

This antagonism can have a class dimension. Many working class men see middle and upper class men as effeminate and 'poofy', and use this as a way of attacking them. There is a real basis to this. We have seen how money and time give greater opportunities for sexual freedom. Moreover, the higher up the social hierarchy a man is, the more real power he has, the less he needs to find a little power in flagrantly lording it over women and effeminate men. The characteristic manner of men of the British ruling elite is indeed far from macho (which is not to say that they are not sexist and heterosexist). This gives the opportunity for populist demagogues of right and left to attack 'degeneracy' and 'vice' in high places. The Jeremy Thorpe case was a (ghastly) case in point. In reality, for working people to use this means of attacking the upper class rebounds straight back, since it reinforces one of the main forms of class rule, the family.

The family divides parents from children, children from each other, and children from other adults. Adult power over young children is inevitable. But the family organises this in a particular way. Children are under the authority of one or two particular adults to whom they are tied by law; they have no choice in this, and this sharply limits their relations with other adults and other children. This gives parental power a large element of arbitrariness. Parents are forced by the demands of childcare to give up much of social life. As a result, parents appear to children as tyrannous, arbitrary, unreasonable, fossilised, while children appear to their parents as wilful, ungrateful, ignorant, in love with change for its own sake. The sexual relation of parents to their children is correspondingly antagonistic. When this sexuality is conscious, as in the very common sexual relationships between men and their daughters, parental power usually makes it exploitative. These oppressive relations between parents and their children tend to be reproduced in the relations between all older people and younger people.

As a means of inheritance of skill, the family divides white from black, since black people inherit part (though only a part) of their disadvantage in the labour market from their parents. This racism of the family can be seen in the reconstruction of the British working class family in the late nineteenth century, when the 'respectable' family of the skilled working class was contrasted with the dissolute family of the underclass and the 'savagery' of the peoples of the empire. White family pride is now built by comparisons with the 'loose' family of the West Indian community. And in consequence, whites (both straight and gay) tend to see blacks as more 'loose', more sexually free. This encourages and legitimises the rape of black women, and impinges on all sexual relationships between whites and blacks.

In all these ways, the family forms an obstacle to making a socialist society. Firstly, the fragmentation that it produces militates against collaboration, against 'common ownership of the means of production'. Secondly, to the extent that the family is responsible for satisfying needs, there cannot be distribution 'to each according to their needs'. The divisions produced by the family ensure that distribution will be radically unequal.

But it is not simply that the family system makes divisions between people who remain passive in the process; not simply that the ruling class seeks to exacerbate these divisions. In each of these situations, the group that comes off best – men, parents, heterosexuals, whites – is drawn into active collusion in the division. This is in part how the family system has continued.

It is not surprising that these power relationships give rise to oppressive needs and pleasures: the need to be straight, the pleasure in being a great stud, in 'queer bashing', in rape. We saw in Chapter 2 how power tends to become sexualised. And in fact so pervasive and important are power relations in our society that sexual desire is to a very large extent centred around power: in many different ways, that is what we get off on.

Where does this leave the traditional socialist principle 'to each according to their need'? The need for social and sexual dominance is real in present day society; but it should not be satisfied by socialism, because it conflicts grossly with the satisfaction of the basic needs of others. It is incompatible with the needs of women, of gay people, of black people, of youth. In a similar way, the need to have more than other people cannot be satisfied by socialism since, with limited resources, this is incompatible with satisfying the basic needs of others.

What are these 'basic needs'? Among them are the need for food, shelter, warmth, physical health; and for collaborative social relationships, for sexual pleasure, for planning the future. These needs arise from our nature, but they are given their form by social development. The project of socialism is not simply to satisfy these needs but to give these needs such a form that they can be satisfied for everyone. This will mean combating divisive needs, and in particular sexual pleasure which is propped upon social power (real or imagined) over another.

This struggle will inevitably be led by those who are the victims of these divisions. But it should be added that sexual desire often inclines the oppressed to collude in their own oppression: to be dominated is as often erotic as to dominate. Many gay men specifically desire straight men, for example, and thus collude in the cult of heterosexuality and masculinity. Oppressed groups have to find ways of combating this source of passivity 'within ourselves'.

To sum up. The family system is not only incompatible with collaboration and solidarity between people. It also prevents the fulfilment of the basic needs of the majority of the population, and fulfils those needs for the rest in an alienated form. Making a socialist society will require making alternatives to the family.

All this may seem rather abstract. But we saw at the beginning of the chapter how the family is already being partly superseded within capitalist society. Many tasks of the family have already been socialised. And those oppressed by the family are already fighting back, are already seeking to make alternatives. These tensions are signs of the real potential for alternatives to the family system.

Public and private worlds

Wouldn't a society without the family be a heartless society, a society where there were no emotional ties, nothing to mitigate the demands of production? Working people have struggled for the family, against the capitalist destruction of it, from nineteenth century Britain to modern South Africa. They have done so because life outside work had been reduced to the tyranny of the boss and the impersonality of the market. Wouldn't socialism without the family be similarly intolerable, similarly spiritually impoverished?

The analogy is misleading. Workers have not, in these cases, constructed alternatives to the family designed to meet their needs; nor have they chosen to submit themselves to the market. Rather, they have been forced to do so by the power of the employing class. And it is generally true that the alternatives to the family supplied by capitalism, from McDonalds to 'guest workers' barracks to the NHS, are geared to the needs of the employing class. They are run in an authoritarian way; they are under-resourced; they are depersonalised by the pervasive ideologies of the self-sufficient family and the free market. They are a sign that 'domestic' work can be socialised; but they are not necessarily a model of how to do so.

Struggles to maintain or strengthen the family have, then, been partly motivated by the nasty aspects of the capitalist alternative. Moreover, to men the family has often seemed an easy option. This was so for example when the male-dominated trade union movement in late nineteenth century Britain fought for a 'family wage', the expulsion of women from the workforce and the reconstitution of the family life and sexual division of labour dislocated by the industrial revolution. The stable family was still a reality among workers' rural cousins and in their grandparents' generation. The men still had more social power than women and were able to fight for a solution which was directly at women's expense. The men had the liberal capitalists on their side, 'wets' who were only too willing to concede what served their interests. The alternative to the struggle for the family would have been the much more difficult and uncertain struggle for socialism.

But the notion of people caring for each other outside of a family structure is not utopian. In spite of the many barriers that capitalist society throws up, even in this society caring and giving relationships are not limited to the family. If you have a job you spend perhaps a half of your waking life with your workmates; you may grow close. Collections for people leaving work, for the relatives of workmates who've died, for people seriously ill or injured, raise significant sums; not significant for what they will buy, but for the commitment they reveal. Personal and emotional commitment and cross-currents run through every sort of association from political parties to charities to amateur sports clubs. The women's movement has shown us that politics need not be impersonal, as well as that 'personal' life is not apolitical.

A socialist society can realise the potential shown in these present-day examples. Commitment to others is in our nature. Socialism hides neither our physical dependence on each other nor our emotional commitment to each other. They are, on the contrary, organising principles of any socialist society.

A socialist society would supersede the family household, and in doing so, would overcome the distinction between impersonal and emotional relationships, between the utilitarian and the giving. Without the institution which gives it sense, the distinction between public and private (which is quite a modern one) would wither away. It would not do this by private life being made into public life as it largely now is: the rule of the market, or the rule of law, the courts and the police. It would do so by private concerns becoming social concerns, being shared, discussed and dealt with with the help of others.

Loving and physical relationships between people close to one another at work or in 'public' contexts would not threaten family monogamy and heterosexuality, as they do today. Nor would a wide web of committed relationships be the cause for jealousy. We are possessive of our spouses and lovers now because they are the only people who are – in theory – committed to us. (The pervasiveness of jealousy indicates how inadequately this guarantees security in practice.) Socialism, in overcoming the oppressiveness and impersonality of the 'outside world', could help to overcome the need for this form of defence. To accuse socialism of creating an impersonal world is to turn the matter upside down.

Beyond heterosexuality

Abolish the family, and won't sex then consist of the sort of sexual relations that now exist outside the family and of quasi-family relationships: alienated, fetishistic, impersonal sex? To be reduced to the world of the gay scene, the disco, the 'singles scene' and prostitution would hardly be progress.

But this is to misunderstand the roots of this sort of alienated and fetishistic sexuality. The problem is not the degree of freedom given by the capitalist market; it is rather the constraints on our sexual capacity created by capitalist society. Our sexual capacity is not fetishised because we actually meet each other as free and equal persons with sexual capacities. Rather, it is fetishised because, while the form of our relation is that of free and equal persons, we are in reality unequal and unfree. It is because a social relationship (the family) which is materially about production and reproduction, takes the form of being about sex, about the exchange of sexual capacities.

How would the constraints on our sexual capacity look in a socialistic society? The problems of population control and inbreeding limit only reproductive sex without contraception. They will still do so in a socialist society. Lack of time and resources may still affect us in a socialist society – socialism is, after all, not an economy of true abundance, even though it can achieve a much faster rate of growth than capitalism.

No doubt a socialist society would try to stop people coercing other people into having sex with them. It may be that in consequence consensual sadomasochism would fade away or be regarded with hostility; we would guess that it is principally a fetishistic or symbolic representation of the link in class society between sex and power, power and sex. It may be, though, that the sensual elements of sado-masochism, pain-pleasure, physical restraint, and the fetishes of leather etc., would survive the disappearance of ritual domination and submission.

But most of the constraints stem from the family, from male and parental power, and from the hierarchy of class. In a socialist society the family and the class system disappear. The remaining constraints that affect our use of our sexual capacity exist openly and are not cloaked in the apparent freedom of the market. In a socialist society we are openly dependent on each other where in capitalist society we appear independent of other people, dependent only on things and on our own capacities. Thus socialism can end the alienation of our sexual capacity.

There is nothing in a socialist economy that dictates heterosexual or homosexual activity, sex by ourselves, celibacy, monogamy or promiscuity. Nor is sex with others any more important than eating with them, playing tennis with them or working with them. By the same token, sexual capacity is not fetishised as it is in capitalist society into identifiable 'sexualities'. Sexual relations are simply a part of everyday life. The other side of this is that what are presently seen as 'non-sexual' relationships – such as those between women, between children, or between adults and children – lose their 'non-sexual' label. There is no call for a market in sex, whether a cash market (prostitution) or a pseudo-market (disco, gay scene, 'singles scene'). There would be no lesbians or gay men in a socialist society – because there would be no heterosexuals.

We don't know what sort of sexual relations or what sort of sexual activities people would engage in in a socialist society. We might guess that they would be kaleidoscopically various. But gay liberation is, in the long run, about liberating the homosexual component of everyone's sexual capacity. A capitalist society cannot achieve this object. A socialist society could.

A horror story?

We anticipate two major objections to our argument so far, which might be summed up by the titles of two books which have become part of modern English anti-socialist culture: Aldous Huxley's *Brave New World* and George Orwell's *1984*. The *1984* objection is this: socialism has been tried and it isn't like that. Socialism in the real world is the dreary tyranny of the state and party bureaucracy, Big Brother, Newspeak, and queueing for shoddy goods: socialism is what they have in Russia and Eastern Europe. There the family still exists, and women and gay people are still oppressed. We will devote the next chapter to answering this argument.

The *Brave New World* objection is this: a socialist society as you have described it is totally alien to us as we now exist. It would mean the end of individuality. We are jealous and possessive of lovers. We want and need privacy. The market may not be wonderful, but at least it gives us freedom from the oppressive closeness of other people. Socialism as we have described it would make of society a giant nursery. The end of the family and of 'private life' would make all social relations incestuous, cloying, stiflingly close.

But human societies are enormously varied. What can be said to be 'natural' for human beings is very limited. Discomfort with the collective socialist society we have argued for does not arise from human nature in general but from our individualist and propertarian nature, formed through living in capitalist society. Thus changes in society and changes in human psychology must go hand in hand.

Any socialist society that emerged in the West today would still be strongly marked by capitalism. This is inevitably the case. We are immediately concerned today with extending choice in how we exercise our sexual capacity, freeing this choice from legal and material restraints as much as possible. We need to extend the socialisation of childcare and domestic labour. We are concerned to abolish special legal powers of husbands and parents; to make it easier for women and men to divorce and for children to get free of their parents, if they wish; and to encourage alternative living arrangements. But we cannot prevent people from forming families if they want to, nor can we immediately abolish inheritance. Nor can people simply 'abolish' their own or other people's fetishised sexual capacities, their heterosexuality or homosexuality.

But this does not mean that we advocate movement at a snail's pace towards a socialism whose consummation is as yet one or two centuries distant. The family, private property and class are intimately connected and cannot be 'dealt with' one after the other. We have given many illustrations of the acuteness of the contradictions of the system of private property and class, family and market, and its crying abuses – including the oppression of gay people. The tensions of the present system are compelling people to look for new ways of life. Nor does capitalism now simply threaten us with 'going on as before'. It threatens us with reaction, a 'return to Victorian values', the 'snuff' movie, with enforced work for the unemployed, with increasing police violence. It threatens us with annihilation through nuclear war.

Its crisis, moreover, is now so acute that gradual and liberal reforms do not even offer a palliative. They break down the old order without offering a viable alternative. Women are freed in law and entitled to equal pay; but nurseries, family planning clinics and jobs are axed. Sex discrimination is illegal, but porn, rape and sexual violence are a rising tide. Gay people can pay highly for inferior entertainment and a competitive struggle for sex in the commercial gay scene; but the gradualist reforms of 1967 are so narrowly hedged about that even this is dependent on the whim of this or that Chief Constable.

This crisis, however, also means that our consciousness, our psychology, is contradictory. It is possessive and individualistic; but it is also social and collectivist. Our sexuality is fetishistic; but we also search for direct relationships with others. People may not want to abandon the family upbringing of kids, but they do want nurseries now. They may not want to abandon marriage, but divorce is soaring. They may not want to abandon privacy, but they want to go out to work, to go to pubs, clubs, discos, to gaze at the shared experience of TV.

Our consciousness is not fixed: it changes social life and is changed by it. No gay person who has 'come out' can deny the possibility of immense and liberating changes in personal psychology; nor should any socialist.

The flip side of the crisis is that a 'realistic', gradualist strategy

– reduction of the gay male age of consent to 18, preservation of the 1967 Abortion Act, more taxes and more borrowing to keep the NHS and the schools afloat – does not even meet people's *immediate* needs. To tackle these needs in the present situation means making a real movement towards socialism. Our slogan is not 'Utopia now'. It is, in Marx's words, 'to set free the elements of the new society with which the old collapsing bourgeois society itself is pregnant'.

4. Gay oppression under 'communism'

This is all very well in theory, you may say, but socialism has been tried and it isn't like that. What it is like is the 'communist' regimes in Russia, Eastern Europe, China, North Korea, Vietnam, Cuba. In all of these countries the family is upheld as the 'basic unit of society'. In all of them women and gay people are oppressed. There is less political freedom than in the Western democracies and therefore less opportunity to campaign for gay liberation. In some of these countries homosexual acts are illegal. Doesn't this prove that for gay people socialism is just as bad, if not worse, than capitalism?

'A bourgeois perversion'

As we have seen, it cannot be assumed that there are gay people in every society. Contrary to their official ideology, however, there are gay people in the 'communist' countries. Because of this ideology, there is very little written about them; but we have some information about lesbians and gay men in Russia, in Estonia and in Cuba, and of gay men in Czechoslovakia, East Germany and China. In all these countries there is a male gay scene, albeit less large and open than in England or similar countries. Particular cafes and bars, public parks, a swimming pool in Prague, private parties and the ubiquitous cottages all provide meeting places for gay people. In East Germany there are gay clubs.

Sex between consenting adults of the same gender is legal in all of the 'communist' countries except the USSR (where male homosexual sex is illegal) and Rumania (where both male homosexual and lesbian sex are illegal). Unlike the UK, the age of consent for gay sex is the same as for heterosex (except of course in the USSR and Rumania) and the same for women as men. It varies from 21 in Bulgaria to 10 in Hungary. Unlike the UK, only the adult can be prosecuted in cases of under-age sex. But there exists the same apparatus of non-judicial control of young people as here. We do not have information on discrimination against gay people in the custody of children. As in the UK, laws of a general nature are used against gay people. For periods since the revolution in Cuba, the 1938 Law of Endangerment was used to imprison lesbians and gay men for 're-education', on the basis of their sexuality alone.

As part of their regime of political dictatorship these countries make all unregistered associations illegal; a gay association would not be registered. A meeting or social gathering of two or more people is an association – so gay groups could be prosecuted. When Italian Radical MP Angelo Pezzana staged a one-man demonstration in Moscow about gay rights, Russian police proceeded to raid previously tolerated gay meeting-places.

As in this country, gay people are oppressed by means other than the law. Official ideology and medical textbooks present gayness as 'sick', 'decadent' or criminal. Otherwise, the media hardly acknowledge the existence of lesbians and gay men, even as objects of ridicule. The KGB told Angelo Pezzana that 'You are the first homosexual we have met; in the Soviet Union there are *none*, and if there were it would be necessary to eliminate them all'. Gay people experience the same everyday oppression from heterosexual people that they do in this country. People refuse to recognise that lesbians exist. Effeminate gay men get abuse from workmates and the public. A lesbian visitor to Latvia found that ordinary people in Riga thought that homosexuality was 'an unnatural practice and must be stamped out'. In China, Vietnam and Cuba gay sexuality tends to be condemned as a part of a general 'puritan' condemnation of sex outside marriage.

In all the 'communist' countries the state controls housing, jobs and movement from place to place. It pursues a rigidly pro-family policy. Single people cannot get housing, but must live with their parents – so many gay people contract marriages of convenience. An additional incentive for this is that to live in a big city in the USSR you must be born there, be married to someone born there, or have an important job there. The gay scene is restricted to the big cities. People convicted of homosexual offences would lose their jobs and be, in effect, deported to a distant province. To cap all, there are virtually no social facilities for anyone, heterosexual or homosexual, except those directly controlled by the Communist Parties or their youth organisations. It is unsurprising in these circumstances that the gay scene is small and secretive in these countries.

Different from the West?

Supporters of the 'communist' regimes see them as socialist or moving towards socialism; on our argument so far, we would then expect to see moves towards gay liberation. Why is the reality so different? We would argue that the reason both for the existence of gay people in the 'communist' countries and – in part – for their oppression is the continued existence of the family together with the satisfaction of many needs by the market or state provision. The latter allow for a degree of sexual freedom; but this is still circumscribed by the family. This leads to a fetishisation of sexual capacity in the 'communist' countries, just as it does in the West.

The family and the oppression of women within it is still firmly in place. Women are legally declared to be equal and are drawn into waged work on a larger scale than in the capitalist countries. But these 'equal' women are expected to be privately responsible for housework and most childcare as well as holding down their jobs. Nurseries are better provided for than in Britain, but are still inadequate and are geared to getting women into waged work. There is greater public responsibility for housing, but it is used as a means of enforcing family life.

The governments also use control of women's fertility as an instrument of economic planning. Contraception and abortion are erratically available. The authorities in several countries have cut the availability of abortion to attack long term problems of labour shortage. Contraception is not much advertised, and, because of bad quality, is erratically effective. In one survey in the USSR 70% of newly married women who did not want a child failed to seek contraception because they were too embarrassed to discuss it with a doctor.

On the other hand, education and health are generally much better provided for by the state than in capitalist countries of comparable development. Cuba has the lowest infant mortality rate and the highest literacy rate in Latin America. Thus the socialist idea of community responsibility for 'domestic tasks' is more developed than in the West even in the poorer 'communist' countries. But it is still definitely subordinate to family responsibility.

The family system as an organiser of a system of unequal incomes is also important. The 'communist' countries only very partially organise distribution according to need. China, in stark contrast to the more developed India, has been able to largely eradicate starvation. But income inequalities are still large in all these countries and continue to grow, particularly in the USSR, Eastern Europe and China. This gives the better off a stake in the family system. And it gives them a stake in inheritance, both of money and of skills.

At the same time, life in these countries is not totally dominated by the family and by family sexuality; it is not like life in a society of self-sufficient peasant family producers, for example (except perhaps in parts of the Balkans, China and Vietnam). To varying degrees, depending on the development of the economy, subsistence is carried out through the market. All households have a wage or other money income. To be sure, wages and prices are fixed by the state, and you can't shop around for bargains or haggle; but you can earn more by working harder, getting promotion, and so on. There is a black market and benefits can be bought by bribery.

There is thus in these countries a degree of freedom in the use of sexual capacity provided by the market, and also by the non-familial aspects of state provision of services and goods (the state sector being relatively more important in the 'communist' than in capitalist countries). This exists in tension with the continued existence of the family and of the state backing for it.

Since the 1960s this tension can be seen in Eastern Europe, as in Western Europe, in the cracking up of the family. The divorce rate has been extremely high, revealing a crisis of sexual relations in marriage. At bottom, these contradictions have the same cause as those in Western society. Technical development has begun to allow and to require the supercession of the family; but the particular form of society requires its continued existence.

Tension between a degree of freedom in the use of sexual capacity and its restriction by the family is thus in some ways stronger, in some ways weaker than in the West. But it has essentially the same result: sexual capacity is fetishised as heterosexuality and homosexuality, and the population divided between a heterosexual majority and a gay minority who are oppressed by them. The political regime of the 'communist' countries has, however, tended to weaken the development of the heterosexual and homosexual identities. The lack of portrayal of gay people in the mass media means that it is less likely that people, especially women, will recognise themselves as gay or even form a gay identity at the level of desire.

For a given level of productivity of labour, there is a limit to how many nurseries and cheap eating places you can provide. These reasons for the perpetuation of domestic work and for market subsistence would apply in any non-capitalist country, however governed. But as we have seen, the states in these countries go out of their way to promote the family and to exacerbate anti-gay practices and prejudices. Why is this?

Stalin and the family

Since all 'communist' countries are to a greater or lesser extent modelled on the USSR, it is important to know how the sexual regime developed there. After the revolution in 1917 in Russia, the Bolsheviks abolished the Tsarist laws against gay male sex. But they were brought back. In 1929 the Uzbek republic established a new law against 'conducting schools of homosexuality', and in 1934 the law against 'pederasty' which is still in force was introduced in the USSR. Homosexuality was dubbed a 'bourgeois perversion', even a 'fascist perversion'. In 1936 abortion was outlawed. 1936 was also the year the USSR adopted a new constitution which formally replaced workers' councils (Soviets) with a parliament; this was accompanied by the Moscow show trials and the extermination of all political opposition to the regime. In the same period divorce was made more difficult and parental authority given the support of the regime. The upper age limit on membership of the Young Communists was abolished, so that this organisation could be headed (as it is to this day) by middle-aged men. And the stream of pro-family propaganda began that still gushes from the Soviet press.

All this was a reaction, a reversal of the earlier policies of the Soviet government. The revolutionary regime had not only legalised abortion, made divorce easy, abolished anti-gay laws. It had also made a real effort to socialise childcare by providing creches, kindergartens, etc; to support the independence of youth from their parents; to establish social laundries and dining-rooms.

Why, then, the change? It's difficult to find a better or clearer account of the attempt to replace the family household, its failure, and the rise of familism in the USSR than in the few pages on this subject in Trotsky's *The Revolution Betrayed*, written in 1936. He wrote:

The real resources of the state did not correspond to the

plans and intentions of the Communist Party. You cannot 'abolish' the family; you have to replace it. The actual liberation of women is impossible on a basis of 'generalised want'.

In consequence a retreat to the family household was inevitable; but

The retreat not only assumes forms of disgusting hypocrisy, but is going infinitely further than the iron economic necessity demands. To the objective causes producing this return to such bourgeois forms as the payment of alimony, there is added the social interest of the ruling stratum in the deepening of bourgeois law. The most compelling motive of the present cult of the family is undoubtedly the need of the bureaucracy for a stable hierarchy of relations, and for the disciplining of youth by means of 40,000,000 points of support for authority and power.

[40,000,000 was the number of families in the USSR in 1936.]

In the first place, the material resources of society were insufficiently developed to replace family production with social production. The USSR, like all other countries which have since had a revolutionary overthrow of capitalism, was poor relative to the advanced capitalist countries. (For this reason the sexual politics of these countries is best compared with Third World capitalist countries rather than, for example, Britain. One of the gains of the 'communist' countries has been that their economic development has generally been rapid relative to comparable capitalist countries. But it has been inhibited not only by the mismanagement of the economies by the ruling elites but by the policy of the capitalist countries: trade boycotts, invasions, and the massive arms production forced on the USSR since the 1930s. To this extent the capitalist countries have been, and are, responsible for the social backwardness of the 'communist' countries.

But this does not explain why the Soviet regime in the 1930s did not honestly explain the difficulties it faced, as the Cuban government (sometimes) does, but should instead promote a cult of the family and the persecution of gay people. This was because the economy and society of the USSR was, and is, ruled by the full-time functionaries of the state and the Communist Party – and not by its people.

In Chapter 2 we argued that classes and castes, which take society's decisions for it, arise because there is a surplus, but not enough to let everyone take enough time off working to participate in taking complex social decisions. In most of the 'communist' countries the level of development means that the majority of the population has to work longer hours than anyone would accept in this country. In such circumstances full-time decision-making specialists – technicians, managers, army officers, ministers and their subordinates, Party secretaries – are inevitable.

However, the existence of functionaries does not necessarily mean a dictatorship. It's not inevitable that these jobs are held for life; that the functionaries are not answerable to anyone other than other functionaries; that they are appointed by patronage; or that they exercise a police dictatorship over working people, suppressing all political opposition. Yet this is what came about in the course of the 1920s in the Soviet Union.

The reason was a series of political errors on the part of the Bolsheviks. They did not expect isolation of the revolution in an economically backward country after the failure of the workers in Western Europe to make socialist revolutions. They had no experience of a corrupt permanent full-time apparatus in their own party or unions; the Tsarist secret police had enforced rotation of officers on them by imprisonment, exile and assassination. The decision of the Bolsheviks to ban factions of ordinary workers ('parties within the party') strengthened the functionaries, who had good reason to take control of the state. They could thereby give themselves a reasonable standard of living, in conditions where the majority of the population was close to starvation. The upshot was that the fulltimers seized power and silenced their opponents.

As a result the Soviet economy is now run by a clique. Without democracy in the workplace or in society at large, it is impossible for working people to discuss and direct production – including the production now termed 'domestic work'. There is thus no 'common ownership of the means of production' in the USSR.

All the revolutions since 1945 have to a greater or lesser extent taken the USSR since the 1930s as their model. After all, the USSR was the rock on which the Nazi armies broke. The Eastern European countries were 'revolutionised' by Soviet conquest, except for Yugoslavia. The Yugoslav, Chinese, Cuban, Vietnamese revolutions found the USSR their principal source of material aid in the immediate aftermath of revolution. And all these revolutions, except those in the Caribbean and Central America, were led by parties which had been thoroughly purged in the 1930s of all those opposed to bureaucratic rule in the USSR and its politics.

What has all this to do with the family and the position of gay people? The ruling stratum of the functionaries is interested in the preservation of the family for several reasons. In the first place, the functionaries' social position is to some extent inherited. To be sure, the key to advancement is political conformity and political patronage. But there is some nepotism. The family upbringing of children affects their education just as it does in the West, and the children of the ruling layer get more access to education facilities than the children of ordinary workers. Sometimes a house or farm can be inherited, legally or extra-legally. The ruling stratum, then, is interested in the defence of the family for the same reason as its petty-bourgeois counterpart in the West: in the inheritance of property and social position.

It is also interested in it for the reasons of 'divide and rule'. Setting men against women and women against men, parents against youth, family against family, heterosexuals against homosexuals, nationality against nationality, the family helps the ruling functionaries to preserve their position. It makes petty power seem natural, and it divides those over whom they have to rule. The Soviet government wanted to silence the film director Sergeo Paradjanov for his support for Armenian national rights; so they prosecuted him for pederasty.

The family is particularly important for the control of young people. Young people were and are the most persistent source of trouble for the rulers, whether this 'trouble' takes the form of apolitical hooliganism, identification with Western youth culture, or of clandestine opposition groups. No housing except for families, the cult of parental authority, forty year old 'Young Communist' leaders, and party control of social facilities, are all means to keep control over young people.

The use of the family for social control is even more important in the 'communist' countries than it is in Britain. This is because of the absence of much of the passivity encouraged by the market. Without significant unemployment the functionaries find it difficult to discipline the workforce. Since enterprises cannot go bankrupt and the state controls foreign trade it's hard to get people to 'compete against the foreign competition'. Since the state owns the means of production and controls prices it's difficult to blame economic crisis on the impersonal market. This 'transparency' of the post-capitalist economy is a great advantage for the workers, but a problem for the ruling elite. We have seen how the middle class in Britain tends to develop a 'sex police' mentality from its job of disciplining the population. The functionaries of the 'communist' countries have an even more difficult job in imposing their discipline, and a family policy correspondingly more virulent.

For the same reason the functionaries have to maintain a political dictatorship in order to hold on to their privileges. Their rule is fragile, as the meteoric rise and achievements of *Solidarnosc* showed. They cannot allow any alternative control or alternative ideology. They therefore cannot allow a women's movement or a gay movement to exist, since this would mean women and gay people beginning to take control of their lives.

The rulers of the 'communist' countries are above all professional managers, fixers. They have always aimed for peaceful coexistence with capitalism, not its overthrow. It is not surprising that they equally aim for peaceful coexistence with the bourgeois family. The kind of popular creative turmoil that would be necessary to devise alternatives to the family (and which to some extent existed in Russia in the early 1920s and in Nicaragua now) is something they cannot manage and therefore abhor. It's hardly surprising that the rise to power of this layer in the USSR and its political imitators should have coincided with propaganda for the family and attacks on women and gay people.

Fidel and the 'maricones'

The attitude of the Cuban government to gay people has been little different to that of the other 'communist' countries. During the first decade of the revolution in the 1960s, there was a purge of gay people (called 'maricones' in Spanish slang) from the teaching and cultural professions where they were said to have a corrupting influence. In this period many gay people were imprisoned, often simply for being gay rather than for specific sexual activities.

Though these large scale purges have ended, the attitude remains. In 1971 the First National Congress on Education and Culture declared that 'The social pathological character of homosexual deviation was recognised. It was resolved that all manifestations of homosexual deviations are to be firmly rejected and prevented from spreading . . .' and went on to call for a series of measures of discrimination against gay people in education, employment and the arts. In 1979 a mass-circulation magazine quoted ads from a New York gay magazine to show gay 'decadence', and claimed that US monopoly capital is planning to export homosexuality on the world market, along with slavery, the arms race and child prostitution. In 1980 when 100,000 Cubans for a variety of motives fled to Miami, Fidel Castro described them as 'degenerates, drug addicts, criminals and homosexuals'. There were indeed among them many lesbians and gay men seeking to escape prejudice and, in many cases, imprisonment for their sexuality. Certainly, not all of the emigrants were opponents of the revolution. As one young lesbian put it, '(In the USA) I have more freedom in regards to being a homosexual. Otherwise, I would prefer to be in Cuba, but I don't want to be in prison.' She reported the predominant sentiment in Cuba that 'it is better to die than to be a homosexual.'

But the Cuban Communist Party does not practise the elaborate propaganda for domestic labour for women and gender-role stereotypes practised by the authorities in the USSR. They do not pretend that they have already achieved the liberation of women. On the contrary, they propagandise in favour of men sharing domestic work and women going out to work; against the double standard of sexual morality and against *machismo*; against presentation of women as sex objects. They struggle to increase social facilities for childcare, laundries, restaurants and so on. They admit that they have fallen short of their targets because of material scarcity and wrong attitudes, rather than glorifying weaknesses as 'true socialism'.

The Cuban government thus promotes 'heterosexuality with equality'. This contradictory attitude can be seen in this official statement of 1975:

Men and women have to be equally free and responsible in determining their relations in the area of their sexual lives. This freedom does not imply *licentiousness*, which degrades the beauty and the relations between men and women. *Relations within the couple* under socialism flow from a different idea; they are established on the basis of equality, sincerity, and mutual respect, and have to be based on clear and advanced ideas about *the responsibility involved in sexual relations – the origin of life and the creator of the new generations*. (our emphasis)

In general the Cuban CP leadership and their co-thinkers in Nicaragua and Grenada had their political education outside of the 'communist movement' controlled by the rulers of the USSR. It is true that they are functionaries; officials are not rotated; and opposition parties and factions are banned. But they strive to involve and mobilise the mass of people in political affairs. This is in stark contrast to the rulers of Eastern Europe, who shun such activities like the plague. Castro is fond of boasting that the majority of the population are armed and trained to use their weapons; if that were true of Poland Jaruzelski's military coup of December 1981 could not have happened. The Cuban leadership, moreover, are by and large revolutionaries, people who were involved in leading the revolution; in the Soviet Union, in contrast, by 1940 the overwhelming majority of those who had been Bolsheviks at the time of the revolution had been executed or sent to Siberia.

The heritage of an independent revolutionary tradition can also be found in Vietnam, Yugoslavia and China, though less clearly than in Cuba. One reason for the repression of gay sexuality in these countries, in spite of these traditions, has been their material dependence on the USSR arising from their blockade by the capitalist countries. Cuba, for example, is for this reason under continuous pressure to tailor its ideology to the Soviet model. The lack of real democracy, even in Cuba, is another reason.

But this does not explain why the 'communist' country most tolerant of gay people is not one where the present leaders were revolutionaries, but East Germany. Why did revolutionary Cuba for twenty years uphold the oppression of gay people? Surely something more than the self-interest of a privileged layer is involved? The Cuban case is the most glaring contradiction, and the best documented. The key to the problem is imperialism.

The regime of Batista, which the Cuban revolution overthrew, was not 'home grown'; it was a puppet of the USA. Cuba was financially drained, and its economy grotesquely distorted by

North American capital. In Havana the North American middle classes enjoyed the vices they condemned at home; alcohol, drugs, illicit sex. Entertainment for tourists and prostitution, both female and male, were large-scale industries. Much the same features could be found in pre-revolutionary Hanoi, in Saigon in the 1960s and early 1970s, in Shanghai and Canton before the Chinese revolution. They can be found on a massive scale in Hongkong and Bangkok today.

This imperialist tourist 'exploitation' is not at the centre of the power relationship between the rich and the poor countries of the world. But it is a symbol of the power of the rich countries over the poor countries, and of the way the regimes of the poor countries kowtow to the rich countries and service the desires of their citizens at the expense of their own citizens. And with this goes fetishisation of the sexual capacities of the dominated people by heterosexual and gay men of the rich countries: the 'passive' East Asian, the 'passionate' Latin American. The racism of this sexuality is obvious.

It would be idle to pretend that the pre-revolutionary gay scene in Cuba or any other of these countries could be separated from this encroachment. A separate gay identity, gay people and a gay scene are not as developed in the indigenous culture of Third World countries as they are in the richer capitalist countries. Foreigners therefore make up a large part of the – almost entirely male – gay scene. The scene is essentially urban; the principal cities were dominated directly by the needs of the foreigners. The gay scene often overlaps with prostitution; the foreigners were the principal clients of prostitutes both male and female. The gay scene thrives in bars, clubs, etc; these were mainly for the rich foreigners. The world of entertainment is one area where gay people are (barely) tolerated in most societies; entertainment was there for the rich foreigners, not the poor natives.

All this makes male homosexuality appear as an enforced export from the imperialist countries. But in reality this is only a minor part of the story. The reason for the greater development of the gay identity in the richer capitalist countries is principally the greater development of the market there. In the Third World, poverty sharply limits alternatives to the family. The contribution that imperialism makes to the development of gay sexuality in these countries is, then, not mainly through tourism but through investment and the development of the market; but here the problem is not too much development but systematic *underdevelopment*.

Nevertheless, the market is now sufficiently developed in all but the very poorest Third World countries for gay people to exist. And the repression of gay people and of gay sexuality in these countries is intense. The massacres of gay people by the Chilean Junta and of those accused of homosexual 'crimes' by the Iranian Islamic government are the tip of the iceberg.

There are now gay movements in several Third World countries. The Mexican gay movement, for example, is not only large but probably the most politically developed in the world. It identifies the oppression of women and gay people in Third World countries with their underdevelopment, and supports the struggles in these countries against imperialist domination. But there was no such gay movement in Cuba or Vietnam or China at the time of their revolutions. Nor were the leaders of these revolutions part of an international movement that supported gay liberation. It is therefore not surprising that these revolutionists identified gay sexuality with foreign domination.

Fidel Castro and his co-thinkers started out as nationalists, as anti-imperialists. They only became 'communists' after the revolution, in response to US trade blockade and invasion. Many of the Chinese and Vietnamese leaders similarly started out as nationalists. Their nationalism made it one of their priorities to clean up the running sore of imperialist exploitation of their country for sex, as in other ways. A certain sexual puritanism is hardly surprising in revolutionists with this background. Nor should we be surprised that this meant repression of a male gay scene that was seen as part of the culture of imperialist exploitation.

Gay liberation and the 'communist' states

The 'communist' countries are not a living refutation of the link we have made between socialism and gay liberation. These countries are not in fact socialist. Gay people in these countries exist, and in the first instance are oppressed, for the same reason as in capitalist countries of comparable economic development: the tension between the family on the one hand and the market and social provision on the other. But to this oppression is added a powerful interest of the ruling cliques in reinforcing rather than seeking to go beyond the family, an interest enforced through the ideological and political monopoly maintained by these cliques.

Socialists and gay people living in the advanced capitalist countries have no cause for complacency in this. On the contrary: most of the countries which are now 'communist' were kept in a state of backwardness by the advanced capitalist countries; and in all of them since their revolutions, economic, social and political development has been held back and distorted by both Cold and Hot War against them by capitalism. The best contribution that we in Britain can make to the problems of the 'communist' countries is to break from the Western military and economic systems, and start to harness a democratically planned British economy to these countries.

There are tremendous tensions within most of the 'communist' countries and of the capitalist Third World countries around the family and sexuality. These tensions, and the demands they give rise to, are not going to wait for the time when these countries have reached the economic and social 'maturity' of Britain or the USA. The fight for gay liberation in these countries already exists. We can learn and benefit from this fight, and we should support it.

5. The future of gay liberation

We think that the liberation of gay people can be achieved in building a socialist society, in which, in the end, there will be neither heterosexual nor homosexual people. But the family system, and the oppression of gay people which stems from it and from the conditions of capitalist society, are obstacles to socialism. Fighting for socialism today, therefore, also means fighting for gay liberation. How to do this is the subject of this chapter.

The gay movement

The symbolic beginning of the modern struggle for gay liberation began on June 28–9 1969, when gay male bar-users in Christopher Street, New York rioted against police raids. These events were a symbol of gay people resisting the attacks of straight society. They triggered the appearance of the Gay Liberation Front (GLF) in the USA, and subsequently of similar organisations in other countries, including Britain. While earlier gay movements had pleaded for tolerance, the Christopher Street rioters and the new gay organisations asserted our right to be gay and to live as gay people, that gay is good!

Advances towards gay rights have always started with action by gay people. The 1967 Act followed a decade of lobbying and propaganda by the Homosexual Law Reform Association. The original demands of the women's movement did not include the sixth demand on sexuality; its inclusion followed the development of lesbian feminist groups and was the subject of sharp debate. The parties, groups and sects of the left were silent on gay rights until the GLF emerged in 1970. The Labour Party proposed a timid measure of law reform in 1982 only because of the influence of the gay movement on the Labour left. Where trade unions have adopted gay rights positions, it has almost always been through pressure from gay caucuses.

It is not only gay people who are affected by gay oppression; but it is gay people who experience this oppression in its sharpest, most inescapable form. Society makes us 'gay people'; by and large, this is not a matter of our choice. There is most likely to be a determined struggle against gay oppression if there exists a self-governing movement of gay people, fighting for our liberation.

The gay scene is places and means by which gay people get to meet each other. The gay movement is gay people organising together to change the world. But the two are necessarily connected. One way in which the world needs to be changed for gay people is more and better social facilities for us. On the other hand, social solidarity and meeting gay people is essential for gay people to acquire the confidence to act together to change things. So gay social life and gay politics shouldn't be separated; to the extent that they are, the politics is much weakened.

Lesbians have an ambiguous relationship to 'gay' organisations which, with the exception of some gay trade union groups, have been dominated by gay men. Lesbians have at various times split from these groups, and have never formed a large part of their membership; nor have these groups organised a large percentage of politically active lesbians. Moreover, many lesbians have developed their sexuality as a part of becoming feminists. It has been easier for them to fight lesbian oppression in women's organisations than to fight women's oppression in male-dominated gay organisations. There are now many separate lesbian organisations. We would see them as part both of the fragmented women's movement and of the fragmented gay movement. They need to be autonomous from both; but their concerns and struggles are part of the common struggle for women's liberation and gay liberation. Somehow the means must be found for common campaigning activity; and in some cases, this joint campaigning has begun to happen. If it is to grow, male-dominated gay organisations will have to make a priority of action against lesbians' and women's oppression.

A strong gay movement, like a strong women's movement, needs autonomy: self-government and freedom from organisational interference. This does not mean that gay liberation is only of concern to gay people, that only gay people will support it. Nor does it mean that the gay movement can avoid taking sides on other political questions; the election of a Tory government, anti-union legislation, the Police Act have all had direct effects on gay rights.

But it has been, and will be, lesbians and gay men who lead the fight against heterosexism. A gay movement organised by a party or sect dominated by heterosexuals, or subject to regulation by the state, would lack the ability to evolve, and to push the struggle for gay people forward beyond what heterosexual people have already accepted. Such a gay movement would also be less able to organise the social solidarity of gay people, and thereby weakened.

For these reasons, socialists, and the labour movement at large, should vigorously defend the right of gay people to organise autonomously – both against the state's conspiracy charges, and against leaders of the Labour Party and trade unions who would like to have only tame gay organisations.

As with the women's liberation movement, socialists must support and help to develop the existing gay liberation movement. To wait until there exists a uniformly 'socialist' or 'communist' or 'working class' gay movement is a recipe for doing nothing about gay liberation.

A manifesto for action

The activity of the lesbian and gay movement starts from the pressing needs and concerns of gay people. We can summarise these as a number of demands:

- An end to discrimination in employment – gay people should have the right to come out at work.
- An end to violence and harrassment – gay people should have the right to come out in public.
- Resources for gay social facilities and for co-operative and social alternatives to the family.
- An end to anti-gay propaganda – gay people should have media and education at their disposal.
- An end to discrimination by the medical profession – there should be alternatives controlled by gay people.
- All women should have the right to choose to have or not to have children, and gay people and children should have the right to live together.
- Women should have economic and legal independence from men.
- Children and young people should have the right to determine their own sexual lives.
- Abolish all anti-gay laws.
- An end to everyday anti-gay prejudice and behaviour.

What are the implications of fighting for these demands?

Ending discrimination in employment
For a gay person to come out is not a simple, one-off act. It is the ability to be open about our sexual identity in a great variety of different situations, including where we work. Whenever this is denied, we are forced to play the heterosexual game, to invent an acceptable life for ourselves, to pretend to emotions we do not have and hide those we do. If we have not accepted our sexuality – and in a deeply anti-gay society it is very difficult to do so completely – this reinforces our self-hatred. But even to the extent that we see our sexuality as valid, disembling inevitably involves self-aggression and suppression of our capacity for sociability. Not to be able to come out is always humiliating and damaging.

The first obstacle to coming out is self-oppression, the lack of confidence that comes from rejection by society and the idea that one's sexuality is 'wrong'. A second is fear of social rejection, of losing one's friends. Part of the role of the gay movement, of gay groups, papers, switchboards, and so on, is to build the self-confidence and solidarity to overcome those obstacles.

Building a gay liberation movement has to start from gay people being proud, confident enough to demand our rights in whatever situation. That strength can only be based on the existence of supportive gay groups. The gay liberation movement intertwines 'personal' and 'political' life; in doing so it reveals its incompatibility with capitalist society.

But there are other obstacles to coming out that social/political solidarity on its own will not deal with. If we come out at work we risk losing our jobs; if we are out on the dole we risk not getting jobs. One way of tackling this problem would be to amend the law to make it 'unfair' for employers to dismiss people on grounds of sexuality, or of open sexuality, wearing badges, and so on. Or, indeed, to introduce a more general anti-discrimination law, like the Sex Discrimination or Race Relations Act.

There are problems with this strategy. Many openly gay people – or people who merely play the wrong gender role – are sacked from their jobs or pushed out of them by the pressure of their workmates. The Tories and the Liberal/SDP Alliance actively exploit this prejudice, as in the Bermondsey by-election; the Labour right-wing, and many left-wingers, back down in face of it. They aren't going to change the law unless it's 'acceptable to public opinion' – that is, unless they're forced to do so by pressure from people who now support the sacking of gay people.

It may seem contradictory, but the way to confront this problem is through increasing the power of workers; through participating in trade union organisation and using this organisation to fight victimisation and harassment of gay people at work. It has been where the trade unions were involved that there have been successes in fighting victimisations. Gay trade union groups have been able to have a real impact on anti-gay prejudice among trade unionists. Women have been able to convince male trade unionists that sexual harassment of women workers by men workers, as well as by foremen and managers, is a trade union issue. It affects the fundamental right of a woman to have a job, it alienates women from unions that are seen to be dominated by men, and it divides the union's membership in the face of the employer's attacks. The same arguments apply with equal force to anti-gay prejudices amongst workers.

Unions, though, have been seriously weakened by the recession and accompanying loss of jobs. People are less willing to strike if they think the management could just fire the lot of them and pick up another thousand or so off the dole queues. This is where a specifically socialist strategy becomes essential – as much for gay workers and trade unionists as for others.

Socialists want to maximise people's participation in social life. Our approach to the problem of unemployment reflects this aim. We want useful jobs for all, and a cut in the working day to free people for other social activities: housework, sex, politics, education, recreation.

The capitalist principle in employment is to hire and fire workers according to profitability and in times of crisis to cut wages, cut jobs and intensify work. The socialist alternative is worksharing with no loss of pay: a cut in working hours, not jobs. This aim can be achieved through industrial action, to impose a measure of workers' power: workers' control of hiring and firing. With these aims in mind it can be seen that the strategy for the unions is not just to protect their present members in work against losing their jobs, but also to organise the unemployed to fight for work – and thus to stop the employer using them as scab labour.

An end to violence against gay people
Coming out in public, trying to meet other gay people, and organising ourselves, we face another threat: everything from

harassment and violence to organised attacks by fascist groups. Lesbians are threatened in addition with the sexual harassment and sexual violence faced by all women.

Relying on the police doesn't seem to be much of a solution. Not only are they soft on rapists, violently anti-gay and infiltrated by fascists, they're also one of the main sources of harassment and violence faced by gay people.

Tougher laws against rape or queer-bashing would have to be enforced by sexist and anti-gay police and judges. The judges have shown their attitude on these matters by largely ignoring the 1976 Act which prohibits cross-examination of rape victims on their sex lives without the consent of the judge; they haven't even bothered to make the defendant show why they should give their consent. This law was tame enough; anything stronger would be treated with equal contempt.

Reforming the police or making them 'accountable' is not likely to solve the problem. The problem consists of the people who work in the police force, and, more precisely, *why* they work in the police force. As long as police work is a job you do full-time for the whole of your working life, a job you volunteer for, the police will attract authoritarian people. (The same goes, of course, for prison offices, customs and immigration officers, and soldiers.) Already the police so regularly exceed their legal powers that part of the case for the new Police Act in England is to extend the powers so that they conform to actual police practice. A law forbidding the police to discriminate against gay people would be largely inoperable because the whole pattern of the police's activity is discriminatory, not just individual police actions. More importantly, the law would simply be ignored. After all, the police themselves operate whatever rules you make to 'control' them.

So what can we do? The Christopher Street riots were an example of unorganised resistance to police violence and harassment. From time to time gay groups have organised defence against attacks on gay people; and gay groups have participated in campaigns against the fascists which aimed to directly prevent them organising their violence. Among black people, particularly young blacks, the need for self-defence against racist and police attacks is now widely accepted.

'Out' gay people are, it is true, a small group. Though much 'queer-bashing' takes place in definite places where the thugs expect to find gay people, and which could, therefore, be guarded, there are also many isolated attacks on openly gay people. Attacks on women are generally on individual women on their own in isolated places.

Consequently, to make self-defence effective we need alliances. There is a real basis for this. The people who attack gay men are the same as those who attack black people, and, often, women. The fascists attack black people and gay people now because they think they can get away with it; in their press they make it clear that if they were stronger they would attack the unions and the Labour Party; if they were in power they would gas or shoot all gay people and labour movement activists. The police already attack union picket lines, as well as being notorious for their attacks on black people. The trade unions and Labour Party, then, should actively support gay, and women's, and black self-defence initiatives. Gay people should seek this support and that of other groups defending themselves against thuggery, fascist violence and police attacks, and should reciprocate with their support.

Arguments have in the past been put forward by some gay groups that this approach is wrong because it is to 'be like our attackers'; rather we should teach them an example of non-violence and peace. We don't think this is practical. There are far more powerful examples pushing our attackers towards violence than any we can provide by turning the other cheek.

Socialism is about everyone participating in all aspects of social decision-making and activity. Policing, and defence against violence are too important to be left to the 'professionals'. In a socialist society, everyone should be involved; the present professional police force should be replaced by a popular militia. But such a militia couldn't be created from above. In fact, the most likely way for it to develop is through the extension of the self-defence activity of the labour movement and of groups like women, gay and black people.

Resources for alternatives

Left Labour councils have been willing to do more about material resources for gay social facilities and for alternatives to family living than about any other issue affecting gay people; for example making grants to switchboards and gay centres and giving some assistance to gay housing co-ops. But these initiatives have been relatively cheap financially, and when the Tories and the Alliance have begun serious use of anti-gay prejudice against them on these issues, the 'soft left' on the councils has backed down. Labour councils everywhere continue to discriminate in favour of nuclear families both in allocation and in the sort of housing they build when they can, even when they have started to make provision for single people.

What we mean by this demand is something rather more serious than a spare and half-derelict building, a small grant to pay a phone bill or support a worker, or a means for the council to ameliorate its housing crisis without compromising its pro-family housing policy. We need gay centres in decent buildings, with space large enough for music and dancing, coffee bars, rooms for small groups, and women-only facilities. Such non-commercial facilities can play a part in developing a less depersonalised gay scene. As we have argued, the fact that access to the commercial scene has to be bought – that it is through the fetishistic medium of money – is not the basis of the fetishistic sexuality that rules the scene. What is offered by free or 'alternative' discos and in non-commercial gay centres is not so different from what market demand elicits, and the way that gay men relate to each other is little different. But the fact that we participate in the commercial scene as consumers, as isolated individuals, means that it is very difficult to challenge or change the way we relate to each other there. With resources directly controlled by us as users, we could and should begin to plan consciously what sort of facilities we need and begin to confront the worst aspects of the sexuality of the scene.

We need decent accommodation and help, properly funded, for women who need refuges to escape domestic violence, and accommodation for those – women and youth – who just want to escape paternal authority in a hurry. The anti-gay, and pro-family, discrimination in council house allocation must be ended.

Some way needs to be found of stopping the discrimination that is practised against gay people – and especially against lesbians – by private landlords and by building societies. Here, too, the law is not a very useful instrument. Regulation of private letting has exacerbated the shortage of housing. The direct approach is simply to abolish the landowner's title. Why should someone receive rent for no reason other than legal title to the property? The squatting movement shows the way forward here. The redivision of houses and streets that squatters have often carried out also points to another type of change. The Ideal Home is built for the nuclear family. Gay people and others need to be able to live together in groups other than couples – and that means a radical change in the layout and design of houses.

People should be able to bring up children and do waged work, so that households with children don't have to be one full-time worker and one 'dependent'. Shorter working hours and better pay would help with this, but we also need a radical extension of nursery facilities, to secure free and well-staffed nurseries available 24 hours a day for all children under school age. The way nurseries are run is crucial, too: without sexist and heterosexist distinctions, and under real popular control. Child allowance should cover the whole cost of feeding, clothing and housing the child, belonging to the child but payable to the adults who assume responsibility for her.

Today a vast amount of the work of caring for the sick and for older people falls on the shoulders of the family – and tomorrow, with the growing cuts in the NHS, the burden will be increased. The burden will fall especially on women, meaning further restrictions on their sexual choices; more lesbians will be trapped in marriage. The disincentive to living openly as gay or outside the family for lack of family support in illness and old age will be increased.

A real transfer of resources to the NHS is needed, confiscating the assets and patents of the drug and medical machine suppliers, and carrying out building with publicly-owned companies. We should aim to secure free medical care for all, and special childcare facilities for ill children. Any or all adults who assume responsibility for individual children should be able to take time off work without losing pay to care for them when they are ill.

We need to extend the personal services developed by capitalism and provide them cheaply or free: low price and high-quality cafeterias, canteens and take-outs, laundries and dry-cleaning services. Present office-cleaning services could be extended to make available cleaning of houses and flats organised on an industrial basis. Another way of carrying out this work would be to encourage the development of 'housework co-operatives', which collectively organise laundry, cleaning, cooking, washing-up and shopping. These can be more efficient than the individual household for dealing with those household tasks that still cannot be done socially, or which cannot be done cheaply or well enough to replace small-scale work.

To provide resources for alternatives is not the same as abolishing the family or compelling people to live outside it. But these changes would make it possible for the family to wither away, as the distinction between private family work and life and public work, education, etc. was eroded at both its ends.

One starting point for achieving these ambitious demands is the existing defensive campaigns against cuts in public services that are now going on in most parts of the country. These campaigns are demanding that public services should get the resources to meet working people's needs. But even in their heyday the NHS, local authority social services, and so on, didn't meet all people's needs. Why not carry the principle of need on to the offensive and demand services and facilities that do meet our needs? 'Lack of money' is only an argument against this if we accept the grossly wasteful and inefficient capitalist management of the economy and the diversion of a large part of production to armaments and luxury consumption.

Another starting point is the squatting movement. Its approach has been to identify the resources needed – empty houses – and then to take them to house homeless people. Workers in Portugal in 1974–6 used the same approach to get buildings for nurseries and other facilities. From the opposite angle, workers at Vickers pointed to resources where they worked that were being wasted in redundancies and arms production, and to how they could be used for socially useful products.

If we start to take some control of economic resources, though, we hit a real problem: resources are scarce, so we will have to find some way of deciding on overall priorities. At the moment the market criterion of profitability decides these questions for society, with the consequences of crisis, waste and austerity that we see around us today. But if people challenge the existing authority and don't set up an alternative, the economy falls apart altogether and people don't have enough to eat. People end up willing to put up with the old order as better than nothing; this is a part of what happened in Portugal in 1975–6 and in Poland in 1981. We will argue below that the socialist alternative is a system of workers' power, and that such a system is an essential part of how to achieve gay liberation.

Ending anti-gay propaganda
How can we end anti-gay propaganda, and, positively, place media and education at the disposal of gay people? Apart from the medical and legal professions there are three main sources of anti-gay propaganda: the media, the churches and morality brigade, and the education system. Gay people have tried to tackle these three in different ways.

In the media we have demanded the right of reply, and lesbian and gay organisations have tried to win this through organising occupations of papers that printed spectacularly anti-gay articles. This is a starting point; but in fact it has rarely produced any result other than a little publicity for the action. On the other hand gay people have tried to produce our own alternatives. In TV and radio we haven't got beyond token 'balanced' programmes. There have been a plethora of gay and lesbian newspapers and magazines, mostly short-lived; the most successful was the old *Gay News*. This should have taught us a lesson by the manner of its demise. It went the way of many privately-owned enterprises: the inevitable conflict between the owner and the workers, insufficient resources, and bankruptcy.

Peter Tatchell, in *The Battle for Bermondsey*, proposes making the National Union of Journalists' *Code of Conduct* an Act of Parliament. This would prohibit discriminatory reporting. But this has the same defects as other law-reform proposals; it asks us to wait for the return of a Labour Government, and if enacted its enforcement would be limited by hostile judges.

Instead, it would be more effective to aim our occupations, pickets and campaigns at the print and media unions who, in the end, could control what appears in the media. We should aim to convince them to use their position to defend the labour movement and oppressed groups, like gay people, by cutting out anti-gay and similar propaganda.

Wouldn't this just replace unaccountable press barons with unaccountable media workers? It's partly because of the way this argument could be used against them that the media unions have so far been reluctant to take this sort of action. But this needn't be so if the action is part of action for a socialist policy towards the media. Such a policy could be open access. This means making media resources available to people as far as possible freely, and where resources are scarce, in proportion to the number of people that will support the particular group which wants access. Gay people would get better media coverage under such a regime than we do now.

Maybe, however, there would be strong support for anti-gay propaganda in the media organised by the churches and the morality lobby, who would then be entitled to media resources.

In the Christian churches, a number of gay groups have begun to campaign against homophobia. We doubt that this approach will make much more headway than it has so far. The Anglican and Roman Catholic churches in particular are privileged and propertied. This makes them natural allies of property and power: they have a stake in the oppression of women and gay people.

Against the morality campaigners, gay people have taken a different tack. We have organised counter-demonstrations to their public events. We have defended people and papers like *Gay News* attacked by them. We should not be afraid to extend this approach to anti-gay events organised directly by this or that church.

These counter-demonstrations have often been small: there are more serious problems than the Festival of Light. Nonetheless, socialists and the labour movement should support such actions. The morality campaigners claim they represent the 'silent majority'; if the only people who stand up to oppose them are small numbers of gay activists it makes this claim look more plausible.

For a government to ban the churches would be tyrannous and self-defeating. For gay groups to try to break up religious services on the grounds of the anti-gay character of the churches would be the same. But churches should be based on the support of living believers, not the patronage of the state or of dead landlords and capitalists who have given them land and money by will. A minimal proposal for law reform would be to disestablish the Church of England, and to abolish the charitable status of religion. In terms of what could be achieved through direct action, the churches should have no exemption from the seizure of land and resources to serve social needs. The wealth and privilege of the major Christian churches is one reason they command such weight as anti-gay campaigners;

attacking these would reduce this role.

Another reason is their role within education. Religion is the only thing legally required to be taught in English schools. 'RE' teachers are quite often also responsible for 'sex education'. Special church schools and church teacher training colleges are maintained, some within and some outside the state education system.

But the education system as a whole is characterised by gender stereotyping in the curriculum, by anti-gay images and by rules which attempt to make children grow up heterosexual. Many gay and socialist teachers are trying to tackle these problems within their schools and Local Education Authorities. But teachers cannot revolutionise the education system on their own. Another and potentially more powerful force is the organisation of school students. The Gay Youth Movement, Young Women's Groups, and the National Union of School Students are the beginners of a movement that could fight for decent education. Their most pressing task inside schools at present is often simply fighting for the right to exist, for students' rights to organise.

To the extent that these groups are concerned with reforming the school from within, heads, right-wing teachers and the government will be able to use the alleged opinions of the 'silent majority' of parents against them. They need to link up with those campaigning against cuts in education services, so that jointly they could also fight for radical changes in the content of education. Successful campaigning needs to stress the need for democratic local control over education, involving students, teachers and the whole local community.

We would argue for education that doesn't oppose children and young people growing up gay, that doesn't deride and trivialise gay sexuality, and that doesn't teach young people to oppress gay people. At the most elementary level, every child has a right to a secular education, and neither parental wishes nor the law should get in the way of that right. The resources of the church schools should be integrated into the state system, and compulsory religious worship and 'RE' should be abolished. The covert arrangements which encourage boys and girls to study 'boys' and girls' subjects' should be ended. Going on the offensive, we need to fight for positive images of gay people and gay sexuality in education as much as in the media.

Ending discrimination by the medical services
In his book on the NHS, *It Makes You Sick*, Colin Thunhurst makes the point that the claims of doctors to a right to control medicine are almost as overstated as those of teachers to control education. Perhaps if we talked about *users* of the NHS rather than about *patients* we would see that there's no reason why the people who use NHS facilities shouldn't have a voice in what those facilities are and in how we're treated.

Gay people's response to medical discrimination has been twofold; to demonstrate at medical conferences on 'the problem of homosexuality', and demand (through the International Gay Association) an end to the World Health Organisation's definition of homosexuality as an illness; and to begin to organise alternatives. In physical medicine women in the women's movement began thinking about and organising women's alternatives some time ago, but this has only begun at all in the British gay movement with the attempts to get alternative information on AIDS not tainted by the scare stories of the straight media. In the gay movement there has long been established an alternative to psychiatry and medical 'treatment' for homosexuality – this has been the work of the voluntary counselling and befriending services.

But such services and alternatives are sharply limited by the small resources of the gay movement; as with other necessary services they need to be financed by the state. Moreover, if we say these services need to be under the control of the people who use them – gay people – shouldn't that be true of the NHS as a whole? This is the framework within which we can confront the particular discrimination that gay people face within the medical services. As with education, we should be fighting for the kind of facilities we need, under popular control – and organising to take the resources we need to get them.

Women's right to control their fertility

The oppression of lesbians as woman and as gay is inextricable; and the oppression of women underlies the oppression of all gay people. The fight for the rights and liberation of all gay people is against the oppression of lesbians as women as well as their oppression as gay. We have therefore included in our demands for gay liberation two slogans of the women's movement which affect all women, not only lesbians.

Lesbians have been in the forefront of campaigns around abortion rights. This was not merely a question of solidarity; they have understood that there is a direct connection between women's right to choose whether or not to have children and women's right to choose to be lesbians. Male power and the family system have subordinated women's sexual capacity to childbearing under the control of men and the state. Women's social and sexual freedom is impossible without control by women over their fertility.

Free contraception and abortion on demand on the NHS is one side of this demand; this requires doing away with the restrictive provisions of the 1967 Abortion Act as well as opposing any new restrictions. It means fighting against cuts and for adequate abortion facilities on the NHS, and to remove anti-abortionists from positions of power to determine resource allocation in the health service. Adequate funding for 'family planning' clinics is needed, and the media trade unions should compel the BBC and IBA to screen public-service ads for contraception and abortion facilities. Young women should be entitled to contraceptives without their parents' knowledge as of right, not just at the doctor's discretion, as now. Women should be free to choose preferred methods of contraception and abortion; and priority in funding medical research should be given to finding 100 per cent safe and 100 per cent effective, and reversible, contraceptives for men and women.

But the other side of the demand is the right to choose to have children. The full provision of nurseries is essential to this; you cannot freely choose to have children, and with whom you will live if you do, if the prospect is imprisonment by childcare. Choice should also involve an end to forced sterilisation and sterilisation without fully informed consent. Discrimination against lesbians and gay men in the custody of children and in adoption should be ended: both gay people and children should have the right to live with whom they choose. We should argue that children cannot be 'corrupted' by gay people, since gay sexuality is itself in no way 'corrupt'. All women should have the right to have children by artificial insemination by donor if they so choose. 'Illegitimacy' and other forms of discrimination against women who have children on their own should be abolished.

Women's financial and legal independence
Women's economic independence from men has a particular importance for lesbians: the economic constraints that keep women tied to marriage produce hardship for those who want to live outside of marriage. There are three main economic constraints: discrimination in housing; discrimination in jobs; and lower pay for women.

The Equal Pay and Sex Discrimination Acts, which were supposed to eliminate pay and job discrimination, have proved completely ineffective. Some hopes have been held out that the Court of Justice of the EEC might do better; and, indeed, the Court condemned the British government for failing to implement equal pay. But this condemnation is toothless; and from this source, too, only very limited results have been achieved. The problem is in part that these laws aim only to outlaw *unfair* discrimination. And the EEC's aim of 'Equal Pay for work of Equal Value' begs the question: how is 'value' to be compared?

As with job discrimination against gay people, the only realistic approach is to rely on the organisation and struggle of ordinary people. For this to be effective, it needs to bring together as many people as possible in common action. This could be done around demands that benefit all workers, especially the worst off.

Equal pay demands the elimination of low pay; this could be achieved by persuading the trade unions to fight for a national minimum wage at the current highest union rate, index-linked to stop erosion by price rises. A policy for equal opportunity and ending job discrimination against all women and gay men, has to start with the demand for useful jobs for all, achieved by worksharing and workers' control of hiring and firing. Only in this way can it be based on the active involvement of all working people, and thus stand a chance of being won.

In the 'communist' countries, drawing women into the workforce and developing nursery provision has all too often meant that it is still the women who do the 'household' tasks, now socialised, while men do 'important' work or are in charge of women. Within the framework of fighting for useful jobs for all and for workers' control, we need to demand a policy of positive action to break down the barriers that have kept women out of traditionally male-dominated jobs.

There is a vast amount of discrimination against married women still operated by the state and the law, especially in the sphere of taxation and social security. And getting married isn't just something that's a 'free choice' for women. Apart from the economic pressures, the media and the education system present marriage as women's natural future. Many lesbians only develop their own sexuality after having married, lived with men, had children – and are subjected to this systematic discrimination.

The institution of marriage cannot be purged of the dependence of women. To 'abolish marriage' by decree is as impossible as 'abolishing religion'. But, like religion, marriage should be disestablished: the state should not lend support or legitimacy to it. The state should cease to register marriages and to prescribe standard terms for marriage or elaborate and costly mechanisms for divorce. People of whatever sex, in whatever numbers, could then enter if they chose into private legal contracts, specifying whatever period they wanted and whatever arrangements for property.

The rights of women should be protected against oppressive terms in marriage contracts (which churches, traditionalist parents, and many men would seek to impose) by a Bill of Women's Rights, which would make such terms legally ineffective. This would limit oppressive uses of marriage contracts, and also have an important influence on people's ideas of marriage. It should protect women's rights to refuse consent to sex; to use contraception and to have abortions; to work for a wage, and to control the use of her wages; to divorce by repudiation or consent and without financial penalties, and to apply for custody of children.

Gay youth's control of their own sexuality

The problems of gay youth and of relations between adult gay people and young people are among the most contentious the gay movement faces. The age of consent, heterosexism in schools, contraception and abortion for young women and the custody of children are issues on which the sex police are particularly active. A popular prejudice is that gay people might 'corrupt' tender minds; a slightly more sophisticated version is that young people are immature and so should be protected from sex in general. It's all too common to hear milder versions of these arguments presented at gay and at socialist meetings – or at least to hear the difficulties of the issues used as an excuse for not taking them up.

We argued earlier for an end to anti-gay propaganda and rules in the education system, and positively for positive images of gay people and gay sexuality in education. Obvious implications are that gay students (and gay teachers) should have the right to come out at school, and that school students should have the right to full information (not censored, anti-gay or religious-tinted information) about sex. Women need access to free contraception and abortion facilities; this applies just as much to young women as to 'adults'.

The right of gay people to bring up children is one of the elementary demands of the gay movement. But what about the other end of this demand: the right of children and young people to choose to live with gay adults? At this point we move beyond equality with heterosexual families. We start to call in question the claim that it's up to adults to decide everything for children and young people, and thus the position of children and youth within the family. This claim underlies the argument for the age of consent, for protection from 'corruption' and all that goes with this.

The family system feeds, clothes, houses and in part educates children and young people. But it also oppresses them. They are subjected to the special and arbitrary power of their parents. Since the mid-nineteenth century in Britain they have been increasingly confined in a narrow and often stifling environment, and denied the right to participate in social, political and sexual life. Isolated from adults and from adult life, their social ignorance and barbarism is at once promoted and used as an excuse to keep them excluded. The population has been divided between 'children' and 'adults', supposedly natural categories which are in fact just as recent and just as social as the 'homosexual' and the 'heterosexual'.

The material functions which the family serves for children and youth could begin to be replaced by resources for social and cooperative alternatives to family living. And conversely, the replacement of the family requires also the liberation of children and young people, freeing them from the development of alternative ways of living.

'Useful work for all' applies just as much to children and youth as to the rest of society, as Marx argued over a hundred years ago. Children and youth of all ages, in so far as they physically can, should have the right to work and earn a wage. The work of children and young people should be regulated to suit physical and mental development, subject to special safety measures, and combined with education. Like the work of adults, it should leave time free for play and relaxation, social and sexual relationships.

People need close and stable social relationships, and we need them most of all when we're young (though right wing ideologues like Bowlby have overstated the importance of certain types of individual attachment). Groups of adults, whether they are the biological parents or not, should take responsibilty for feeding, clothing, housing and giving emotional support and some basic education to children up to the age of puberty. The adults who take that responsibility should be prepared to stick with it, and the state should register their responsibility. But children should be able to 'divorce' their parents or their responsible adults if they choose. It should be up to the child whether or not to divorce the parent, not a matter for professional social workers to replace parental tyranny with state tyranny.

Later we will argue for the reorganisation of the state on the basis of a system of workers' power. In such a system the integration of education and work, and children's and young people's involvement in work, would make it possible to abolish the age of majority. The involvement of young people in social decision-making would then progress gradually as their education and their participation in work increases.

It follows from what we have already said that we favour the abolition of the age of consent. Children and young people do not need to be protected from sex. Both the sexologists' and the anthropological evidence shows that children are just as sexual as adults. If a person, whether adult or child, didn't really agree to a sex act, or wouldn't have agreed if they knew what was involved, then the other person would be punished for rape, sexual assault, or fraud. The same applies if there was only 'consent' because the other person had power, such as a teacher, boss, husband, or a parent: in our society father-daughter incest is one of the commonest forms of child abuse.

The real content of the age-of-consent laws is parental and state power over children and youth. They are used to repress deviant sexuality in young people and to try to make them grow up straight. In a society where sex has become such an important symbol of freedom, the age of consent laws are very important ways of labelling children and youth as necessarily unfree; they should be abolished. For adult-dominated gay organisations to fight for equalisation of the age-of-consent laws at sixteen is to scab on gay youth, and, indeed, on heterosexual youth who are put in 'care' for breaking these laws. Abolishing the age-of-consent laws wouldn't stop people being punished for sexual assaults on and exploitation of children and youth. The question of genuine consent would be, as it is now with adults, one of fact.

These changes may seem very radical, but they can be won. The starting point is young people organising themselves, in school students' unions, political youth groups, young women's groups, gay and black youth groups. Such organisations begin to actively involve young people in changing society and fighting for their own liberation. Their fight to break down the power of parents, teachers and the state has the same aim as women's and gay people's fight for liberation. It is part of the alternative.

Abolishing anti-gay laws

In Chapter 1 we listed some of the anti-gay laws that exist in this country. These are not just laws specifically directed against gay people; many are intended to bolster marriage and sexual 'morality' in general. Some that apparently have no connection with sex at all have been used against gay people – as 'blasphemous libel' was against *Gay News*. Gay life since the Sexual Offences Act 1967 has shown rather sharply that just liberalising those laws directed specifically against gay people still leaves the police a fair armoury against us. Equalising the law (even so as to abolish the public policy against homosexuality) would, for instance, leave it possible to prosecute gay lonely-hearts ads as 'conspiracy to corrupt public morals' – provided heterosexual lonely-hearts ads were similarly prosecuted (something which is by no means inconceivable). The fact that anti-gay laws also repress other types of consensual sexual activity should make them more rather than less easy to campaign against.

What changes should be made in the law? Abolish the crimes of buggery and gross indecency, and 'procuring' those crimes. The anti-prostitution laws simply victimise prostitutes and gay people. They too should be abolished, as should 'keeping a disorderly house'. Abolish 'outraging public decency', conspiracy to corrupt public morals, and blasphemy, and abolish any power of the courts to create new crimes or revive old ones. 'Soliciting' and 'importuning' should not be equalised but abolished.

Obscenity laws are used against gay people, the women's movement, and others who want to discuss the politics of sex. They ban some material which is simply erotic, and some gay magazines which provide ways for isolated gay people to get contacts. But much of the increasing volume of porn incites violence against women, and legitimises rape. The various anti-porn and censorship laws should all be abolished, and replaced with laws prohibiting depictions of women coerced into sex or the objects of male domination, which imply that they like it that way, or that men have a right to coerce women.

A genuine reform of anti-gay laws would declare that there was no public policy in favour of marriage or against any form of consensual homosexual activity; that a person's sexuality was irrelevant to deciding the question of custody of children; that homosexual advances not amounting to attempted rape were not provocation to murder. And positively, it would declare that discrimination on grounds of sexuality was contrary to public policy. A good way to lend point to this declaration might be to make discrimination a new tort or civil wrong, for which one could sue, like assault in the present law. Whether it would achieve much practical good, given the present judicial system, is another matter.

Changes in the law such as those we have proposed would undoubtedly be sabotaged by the judges. And it may seem utopian to expect many of the measures we have argued for to be legislated by a British parliament or local council and implemented by Whitehall or the local authority bureaucracies. At this point we return to the central problem of strategy for socialism – the problem of the state.

The way forward

A socialist society cannot be legislated into existence. But whether society develops towards socialism or away from it depends on the organisation of the state.

For the state in the West and in the capitalist Third World, money talks. It talks openly and legally through the profit-making media, through political contributions to right wing parties, through lobby organisations like the British CBI and the Institute of Directors. That money talks is the fundamental principle of the English legal system: a highly paid lawyer can make a case for anything. Money talks secretly and quasi-legally through direct bribery, through directorships for former civil servants who advised the right way, through groups like the Labour Committee for Transatlantic Understanding. Money talks when the value of the pound collapses, and when the IMF imposes austerity measures. But above all, it talks through the dislocation and misery caused when investment is withheld from an area, an industry or a country.

To move towards socialism we need a state system in which money doesn't talk, one which responds directly to the needs of working people. This would be a system of workers' power. The experience of post-capitalist states, which we discussed in Chapter 4, has many lessons here. We would argue for local government by bodies of delegates elected by workplace or local assemblies which meet frequently and can remove their delegates; and national government constituted by the delegates of those delegates, also recallable. A state of this kind would be able to take the inevitable difficult decisions on the allocation of scarce resources from the standpoint of working people. Within it gay people could win the fight against anti-gay prejudice and for decisions that took our particular needs into account.

There should be complete freedom of political parties, trade unions and other organisations of working people, including women, black and gay people; but disenfranchisement of those who live off the profit from other people's work. People holding full-time positions in the state should be rotated; and state full-timers should be excluded from voting. Large enterprises and banks should be publicly owned and the right to receive rent for land you don't occupy abolished.

Such a system is incompatible with Parliament as it now exists; with the authority of the Crown, with the rule of the judges dubbed the Rule of Law. The present powers of the judiciary are incompatible even with minimal local democracy, as we have seen in the 'Fares Fair' episode in London – let alone with active popular involvement in decision-making. A minimal democratic reform of the judiciary would be election of judges or political controls on their appointment, as is partly the case in the USA. A socialist regime would have to radically reduce the powers of judges, limiting them to commercial disputes in the remaining private sector. Crimes and small individual disputes would be dealt with in local assemblies. This would be a great advantage to gay people; in local assemblies one can argue with prejudice as one cannot argue with the judge.

To introduce such a system would be a revolution, in the sense of a complete change of the constitution. It would undoubtedly meet with resistance – from senior civil servants, from army officers, judges, lawyers, police, landlords, business. It may be that a socialist government elected to parliament could bring about such a change without a civil war, or it may not be. Certainly, to bring about such a change, and to overcome the resistance of the vested interests opposed to it, would need direct action on a massive scale by working people. The action of working people – the large majority of the population of Britain – would be, after all, the foundation of a system of workers' power.

The conclusion is that it would be foolish and ultimately self-defeating to stake all on the election of a socialist government. Socialist change can only come about through the initiative of millions of working people; voting is not enough. Conversely, we can begin to achieve socialist changes in society, and make a socialist government more likely, through seeking to build the active involvement of as many people as possible in fighting for the particular changes we seek. The logic of such campaigns is that they need a regime of workers' power to achieve durable results; but they also begin to create such workers' power now.

It is from this standpoint that we put forward the demands for gay liberation today. Our main task is to build campaigns, involving as many people as possible, that begin to assert the power of ordinary people. This is as true of fighting for gay liberation as it is for any other aspect of socialism.

From one standpoint our proposals may seem crazy and extreme: 'You'll never get a parliamentary majority for that!' But they can be won, if we build a powerful enough campaign for them, if we convince working people to fight for them. It's because our job is to convince ordinary people, not Home Office bureaucrats, that certain sorts of compromise are foolish. You'll never convince bureaucrats and Tories. But to compromise on some demands – like the age of consent – is to admit that the case against *any* reform has weight. It is an admission that you are wrong in principle: no one will be convinced.

Some may argue that these campaigns are less important than changing our lives now. Isn't the best way to get our ideas across to live like socialists, to reject oppressive ways of living as gay people? Particularly since the youth revolt of the late 1960s and early 1970s, many people, both gay and non-gay, have sought to live in a way radically different from that prescribed by straight society. The manifesto of the Gay Liberation Front in 1971 argued:

Linked with the struggle to change society is an important aspect of gay liberation that we can begin to build here and now – a NEW, LIBERATED LIFE-STYLE which will anticipate, as far as possible, the free society of the future.

People have tried to construct alternatives to the family, the isolated couple or the solitary bedsit. There have been experiments with large households, with parts of the housework and childcare shared, and sometimes incomes shared too. There has been the attempt to reject, not just marriage, but 'coupledom'. This has not been done simply (or mainly) by not being sexually monogamous, but by trying not to privilege one friendship above all others just because it's sexual, and thereby excluding real caring from the others. Some people, particularly women, have consciously rejected parenthood.

The fact that so many people have attempted to make new lives in this way, often against enormous obstacles, is eloquent testimony to the crisis of the family. People desperately need to find alternatives. And these experiences demonstrate that we are not family-oriented by nature. Both the successes and the failures have been important in enabling us to imagine what a more systematic alternative might be like, one without the obstacles. Much of what we say in this book would not have been written without these experiences. It is therefore false to argue, as some socialists do, that lifestyle experiments are 'irrelevant to the concerns of the majority of workers'.

But the obstacles are enormous. Many communal households founder, wrecked by sexual jealousy, becalmed in a Sargasso Sea of dirty washing up, run aground on lack of commitment. Underlying the problems are the ways in which capitalism organises our domestic lives. Private incomes are hard to share once you get away from the standard way that they are shared in nuclear families. Housework and childcare is hard to share once you abandon the usual arrangement where one person is saddled automatically with this work because of her sex.

Moreover, where we try to change our lives on an individual basis, we come up against the interests of others. In general, women cannot persuade men to take equal responsibility for housework because men have a real stake in not doing so. We think that men should take this responsibility now, but we believe that this will only come about on a substantial scale as a result of making 'domestic' work a social responsibility.

We are also under tremendous pressure from the nastiness of the outside world to take refuge in easy solutions which might seem to provide compensation: the 'power' of parenthood, the 'security' of coupledom. And on top of this are the difficulties of fighting the expectations and needs we grew up with.

All these kinds of pressure ensure that 'alternative lifestyles' now remain limited to a small minority of the population. The measures we have already outlined are thus necessary to make alternatives possible for the majority. For these reasons a strategy which centres on or relies on changing lifestyles can't be a strategy for socialism and gay liberation. Even if it were possible to remould people's consciousness in the 'appropriate' way through propaganda alone, the material obstacles ensure that most people could not change their lives. The family has real roots in our society as well as in our heads.

To change these conditions requires a political movement of millions of people, most of whom won't – at least at first – be involved in new lifestyles. A lifestyle strategy, on the other hand, is elitist both in that it relies on the 'enlightened' telling people how they should live, and because in practice it is now possible only for a minority.

The proposals we made above may seem very radical, but none of them abolish the family. They are proposals for making available material alternatives to the family system, and for securing the liberation of women and youth, as well as for ending the present discrimination against gay people. Any or all of these proposals can be supported by people who personally wish to go on living in families.

Nevertheless, the reality of the crisis means that a minority will be forced to live outside at least some of the norms of straight society. This is true of gay men but much more true for lesbians. Capitalist society has niches for the single man, and the male gay scene is relatively well-developed and serviced by business*men*. But lesbians have consciously to make their own social support network, their own living arrangements.

Promotion of alternative lifestyles does not amount to a strategy. But alternative lifestyles are necessary for some of us to survive in capitalist society, and they contribute to the vision of socialism.

Gay liberation and socialism will only be achieved through the active involvement of millions of working people in fighting for them. To build such organisation, we have to start from what we have achieved already. We have argued that socialists have to support the existing women's and gay movements; in the same way, gay people and socialists have to start with the existing organisations working people have built up: the Labour Party and the trade unions.

It is true that these organisations are desperately weak at actively involving their activists, let alone the millions of working people who passively support them: ten million trade unionists, eight and a half million Labour voters. All Labour ever wants you to do is vote, and, if you're a member, pay up and perhaps turn out at election time. The trade unions keep their social policies for hole-in-corner meetings and badly circulated journals; when strikes are organised, it's out the gate, back home and let the officials get on with it. We are now paying the price of this weakness in ten years of Tory government.

A connected problem is that 'democratic' Labour and trade union leaders tend to have the same attitude to internal opposition as their counterparts in the 'communist' countries. They also tend to have the same attitudes to women, the family, and gay people. This is hardly surprising, since they are the same social group. Bureaucrats East and West have a similar view of the world, however much they may ritually denounce each other.

But the Labour Party and the unions are what we have built so far. They do begin to organise working people, however limitedly. They could do more, and if they did they would be stronger. Trying to start again from scratch, when these organisations exist, just bypasses the problems without solving them. It's also a recipe for isolation and ineffectiveness. Gay people can defeat victimisation at work – if the unions will help. We can win larger changes – if ordinary people, who now vote Labour or are trade union members, are convinced to fight for them. In this way people begin to involve themselves in political activity – and so change the unions and the Labour Party.

Political positions taken by the official bodies of the labour movement are influential. Public opinion on abortion rights was shifted strongly when the Labour Party and TUC adopted pro-abortion positions. Conversely, when the Labour leadership stabbed Peter Tatchell in the back, there was an open season of homophobia not only by the press but also by working class bigots in Bermondsey. This is another reason for fighting for gay liberation in the labour movement.

All working people do, in fact, have an interest in gay liberation: from the small matter of ending a division that sets working people against one another, to the massive problem of dealing with the crisis of the family. This means that the Labour Party and trade unions, claiming to represent the interests of working people, need to commit themselves to support for gay liberation: to demands on the state and the employers, to fighting anti-gay prejudice among their members, and to supporting the organisation of their gay members.

The tradition of the Labour Party is of promotion of the family, even though this was somewhat toned down in the sixties. It is not surprising to hear Neil Kinnock commenting during the onslaught by the Labour Party leadership and the press against Peter Tatchell, 'I'm not in favour of witchhunts but I do not mistake bloody witches for fairies' (as quoted in the *Daily Express*), and reminding readers of the *Sunday Times* that he is on the 'balls wing' of the party.

However, the impact of women and gay people organising both outside and inside the labour movement has meant that this traditional pro-family policy is now strongly contested. It has meant that the Labour Party now has a policy on gay rights, even if a grossly inadequate one. 'Labour's Programme 1982' committed the party to reduction of the gay male age of consent to 18, repeal of the law on soliciting, amendment of the employment legislation to bar dismissal for sexuality, and legislation to outlaw discrimination on grounds of sexuality. The 'Campaign Document' manifesto of March 1983 contained a watered-down version:

We are concerned that homosexuals are unfairly treated. We will take steps (along the lines of Labour's Programme 1982) to ensure that they are not unfairly discriminated against, especially in employment and in the definition of privacy contained in the 1967 Act.

It is a major step forward to have any pro-gay policy at all. Yet no campaign has been mounted to promote even this feeble policy. What is 'fair' discrimination with which 'unfair' discrimination is contrasted? The age of consent for men at 18 is still discriminatory – and would be 'illegal' under the anti-discrimination law! Change employment law to bar sacking for sexuality, but no doubt permit it for inability to work with other staff, for wearing badges, or for conviction of a sex offence.

In local politics, some left-led Labour councils have introduced a non-discriminatory employment policy, and given some support to gay groups. Where this has been done determinedly and unapologetically, it has had an important impact on popular ideas. And the self-organisation of lesbians and gay men inside the Labour Party and Young Socialists has expanded rapidly. But the sex police remain well represented inside the Labour Party. Labour-controlled Barking Council sacked Susan Shell from her job in a young women's home solely for being a lesbian. And in Coventry the Labour City Council has banned a gay festival on the grounds of 'public decency'.

In the trade unions, there are now gay groups in the AUT, CPSA, G&MWU, NATHFE and NUT, in NUPE, in Post & Telecommunications and the print industry. The Conferences of NALGO, CPSA and NUPE have adopted gay rights policies. The 1983 Conference of NALGO in the Isle of Man voted to boycott anti-gay conference venues, and half the delegates joined in a demonstration against the anti-gay laws on the island. NALGO has also produced the first union pamphlet on gay rights. These victories have, in turn, given a boost to gay self-organisation in the union. But the union leaderships and many full-timers, even in 'progressive' unions, drag their feet on these, as on other 'social' issues.

The way in which these changes have taken place is a practical example of the central arguments of this book: the connections between gay and women's liberation, between gay liberation and workers' power. Gay self-organisation in the labour movement, and the gains in policy on gay rights, have in most cases been made where women's organisation and demands have blazed a trail. It has been parts of the left in the movement, who also want the movement to become more democratic and militant, who have supported gay rights motions and actions. The right wing supporters of Parliamentary Sovereignty, the Tories and the dictatorship of the full-timers have opposed them. And women's and gay organisation have (albeit informally) been a major element in the development of a campaigning left within the Labour Party and trade unions, pushing for a movement which does actually fight for working people's interests.

The experience of the battle for gay rights in the labour movement shows that the way to win is to convince the ordinary members and to do this you need consistent policies. If you merely lobby the bureaucrats, whether of the Home Office or of the union, and tailor your policies accordingly, they'll simply ignore you.

This strategy may be criticised on the ground that political campaigns and social provision leave untouched the most immediate problem of gay people – the day-to-day oppression that we experience from ordinary heterosexuals with whom we come into contact. Others may feel that changes in the structure of society can only take place if anti-gay prejudice has already been eliminated or at least diminished. How, then, do we combat heterosexism, and how does this fit in with our strategy?

We have argued that gay liberation is in the interests of all working people, including heterosexuals. It is this that gives us confidence that heterosexism can be successfully fought. But we have also seen that prejudice against gay people is deeply rooted in the organisation of our society and linked to the organisation of people's sexuality itself. Thus while we seek to collaborate with heterosexuals in the fight for gay liberation, it is also necessary to fight hard against heterosexism in all its myriad forms.

A lot can be, and is being, done by individual gay people and socialists taking up instances of homophobia and arguing against anti-gay ideas. But simply urging individuals to do this more – or urging gay people to come out – isn't the key to making these things happen more widely.

More gay people will come out only if they have the support of gay organisations, and if they are confident of not being sacked or attacked when they do so. This is why, for example, trade unions must support gay people coming out at work. Discussions about gay sexuality occur when the issue is raised in trade union branches or by demonstrations for gay rights. Campaigns to change laws, as well as the changed laws themselves, change attitudes. The stand of the Labour GLC has done much to counter anti-gay ideas; a socialist government could do much more. And the existence of a lesbian and gay movement, with backing from organisations of working people, putting forward the idea that 'gay is good', is the most powerful rebuttal to heterosexist prejudice. We need to fight individuals' anti-gay prejudice. But this is not a task separate from the organisation and campaigns we have discussed in this chapter.

What should we be doing right now to achieve gay liberation? To be sure, various lesbian and gay groups are working in most of the areas we have outlined. But shouldn't we be concentrating on something? Does the Thatcher government mean that we should lower our sights, and concentrate on defending the toleration that we've got now, and on defending individuals attacked by the sex police? Or can we go on the offensive and campaign for serious law reform?

The most striking feature of politics today is its instability. A book which discusses the immediate tactics for gay liberation is in danger of being out of date by the time it appears. Up to now the present government has not made a serious concerted attack on gay people, as it has on the unions. Rather, attacks have been left to the 'private enterprise' of local police forces and local authorities, individual judges, individual newspapers. Some limited gains have been made by legislation to extend the 1967 Act to Scotland and Northern Ireland through the European Convention on Human Rights. If this situation continues we would argue that the most useful thing we could do is to mount a campaign for law reform of a new kind – for a *Lesbian and Gay Rights Bill*.

Such a Bill should declare in its preamble the equal value of lesbian, gay male and heterosexual activity, and proclaim the purpose of eliminating legal discrimination and anti-gay laws. It should start by abolishing the anti-gay 'public policy' of the law. It should specifically override the caselaw of discrimination in the custody of children, dismissal from work, provocation to murder, and immoral contracts, and stipulate that sexuality shall be irrelevant to these questions. It should make discrimination on grounds of sexuality actionable as a civil wrong, so that people can seek redress and damages in the courts, as for a broken contract, for example. The Bill should simply abolish all the principal gay crimes, without inventing an additional age-of-consent law. The only new crime it should create is homosexual rape.

The value of a campaign like this would be symbolic as much as practical. But by attacking the legal symbols that say 'gay is bad' we could disorganise the sex police. The 1967 Act encouraged ordinary people to think that gay people have rights; a vigorous campaign aimed at the law, particularly one involving the organisations of the labour movement, would promote the same idea and could reverse the current erosion of what we *have* got.

But the present situation is an unstable one. The government may win a few more victories and deepen its crusade for

Victorian values with a more open and centralised attack on gay people. In that situation we would be forced on to the defensive; we would really have to lower our sights and fight to defend what we have got – limiting ourselves to defending individuals against victimisation, for instance, or defending the 1967 Act against repeal. Or, looking at matters more optimistically, the labour movement may turn the tide against Thatcherism and in a year's time we may have a Labour Government. In that case we could not only campaign around a model Bill, we could go on the offensive on a good many of the other issues we have discussed.

There are other possibilities. But the instability of the present political situation is in itself good grounds for optimism. We are at present in the midst of a historical crisis of the old order under which gay people have been oppressed. This crisis may end in reaction and even in the destruction of civilisation through nuclear war. But it may equally, if we find the way, end in socialist change and an end to the division between heterosexual and gay people.

Lesbian and gay organisations

Information on organisations can be obtained from local lesbian/gay switchboards, from Lesbian Line on 01-251 6911 (7–10 pm Tue–Thurs, 2–10pm Mon and Fri), or from London Gay Switchboard on 01-837 7324 (24 hours).

Specifically socialist lesbian/gay campaigning organisations are:

Labour Movement Lesbians, A Woman's Place, Hungerford House, Embankment, London WC1

Lesbian and Gay Young Socialists, 39 Chippenham Road, London W9 2AH

Labour Campaign for Gay Rights, 21 Devonshire Promenade, Lenton, Nottingham NG7 2DS

Within the trade union movement there are the lesbian/gay trade union groups listed in Chapter 5, and the Gay Rights at Work Campaign, 7 Pickwick Court, London SE9.

Further reading

Chapter 1

There is a wide range of material on the position of gay people in modern society. On the legal position, the police etc., Paul Crane's *Gays and the Law* (London: Pluto Press, 1982) covers all areas in some detail, as does S. Cohen *et. al.*, *The Law and Sexuality* (Manchester: Grass Roots Books, 1978). The National Council for Civil Liberties, the Gay Rights at Work Campaign and the Campaign for Homosexual Equality have produced pamphlets on gays in employment. The CHE has also published pamphlets on the law and on 'queer bashing'. The Gay Teachers Group and The Socialist Teachers Alliance have published a pamphlet on gays and education. On gays and nazism, see H.Heger, *The Men with the Pink Triangle* (London: Gay Men's Press, 1980); and on gays and contemporary fascism in Britain, the Gay Activist Alliance's *Anti-Fascist Handbook* (1978).

On the experience of gay people in society in general, the *Gay Liberation Front Manifesto* (1971) and Don Milligan's *The Politics of Homosexuality* (London: Pluto Press, 1973) are still relevant and also deal with issues we discuss in later chapters. The same applies to *Homosexuality: Power & Politics*, edited by the Gay Left Collective (London: Allison & Busby, 1980), David Fernbach's *The Spiral Path* (London: Gay Men's Press, 1981), Guy Hocquenghem's *Homosexual Desire*, (London: Allison & Busby, 1978), Mario Mieli's *Homosexuality and Liberation* (London: Gay Men's Press, 1980) and Susan Tyburn's *Breaking the Chains* (Toronto: International Socialists, 1979).

We would not necessarily endorse the political views of any of these. There is a good deal of academic sociological material on gay people in modern society; *The Making of the Modern Homosexual* edited by K. Plummer (London: Hutchinson, 1981), contains discussions of several topics and an extensive guide to further reading in this direction.

Chapter 2

The theory of sexuality in general, and of homosexuality, is also a much-studied subject. On sexuality in general, H.A. Katchadourian and D.T. Lunde's *Fundamentals of Human Sexuality* (New York: Holt, Rhinehart & Winston, 1972) though now somewhat dated in places, assembles a good deal of material in an accessible form. On homosexuality, Martin Dannecker's *Theories of Homosexuality* (London: Gay Men's Press, 1981) is a useful and concise overview, though we would not agree with all of his conclusions. Michel Foucault's *History of Sexuality*, Volume I (London: Pelican 1981) has been, we would think undeservedly, very influential with some theorists of sexuality in this country; on some of the philosophical problems with this sort of theory, Perry Anderson's *In the Tracks of Historical Materialism*, (London: Verso, 1981) is useful.

On biology, evolution and human nature, R. Leakey and R. Lewin's *People of the Lake* (London: Penguin, 1981) and Leakey's *Making of Mankind* (London: Michael Joseph 1981) are accessible popular accounts of human evolution and its possible social implications; on evolution, biology and society in general the material in *Against Biological Determinism* and *Towards a Liberatory Biology*, collections of papers edited by Steven and Hilary Rose (London: Allison & Busby, 1982), contains fascinating explorations. Norman Geras's *Marx and Human Nature* (London: Verso, 1983) argues in detail the reasons for believing that Marx did, and marxists should, accept the idea of a transhistorical human nature.

C. Ford and S. Beach's *Patterns of Sexual Behaviour* (London:

Greenwood Press 1980), though now relatively old, covers the widest range of primitive societies. The classical marxist theory of the origins of women's oppression is that of Engels in *Origins of the Family, Private Property and the State* (a current edition is that published by Lawrence & Wishart, London: 1972). Some of the contrary anthropological evidence is discussed in Leakey & Lewin (*op. cit.*) and in the Keenan, Bonte, Harris and Young papers in *The Anthropology of Pre-Capitalist Societies* edited by Joel S. Kahn and Josep R. Llobera (London: Macmillan, 1981).

On homosexual activity in historical societies, Vern L. Bullough's *Sexual Variance in Society and History* (Chicago: University of Chicago Press, 1976) is the widest-ranging discussion. On more specific areas and periods, K.J. Dover's *Greek Homosexuality* (London: Duckworth, 1978), John Boswell's *Christianity, Social Tolerance and Homosexuality* (Chicago: University of Chicago Press, 1980) on Roman and medieval Europe, Alan Bray's *Homosexuality in Renaissance England* (London: Gay Men's Press, 1982) on the sixteenth to the early eighteenth century, and Jeffrey Weeks's *Coming Out* (London: Quartet, 1977) and *Sex, Politics and Society* (London: Longman, 1981) on the nineteenth and twentieth centuries, are all more detailed. All of these books take or assume different views on the origin of the modern category 'homosexual'; for others, see Mary McIntosh's and John Marshall's essays in *The Making of the Modern Homosexual*, edited by K. Plummer (London: Hutchinson, 1981) and John D'Emilio's article in *Desire: the Politics of Sexuality*, edited by Ann Snitow, Christine Stansell and Sharon Thompson (London: Virago, 1984). On capitalism and the family Michael Anderson's *Approaches to the History of the Western Family* (London: Macmillan, 1980) provides an overview of the subject; we have been influenced also by Wally Secombe's article on 'Marxism and Demography' in *New Left Review*, issue 137.

On alienation and fetishism we have largely followed the account in G.A. Cohen's *Karl Marx's Theory of History* (Oxford: Oxford University Press, 1978). On the specificity and 'naturalness' of women's sexuality there is a great deal of discussion. *Sex and Love: New Thoughts on Old Contradictions*, edited by Sue Cartledge and Joanne Ryan (London: Women's Press, 1983) and *Desire: the Politics of Sexuality*, edited by Anne Snitow *et. al.* (London: Virago, 1984) are recent collections of feminist essays. Section 1 of *Desire* deals specifically with the question of 'naturalness' and fetishism. On the relation of this to a specifically lesbian sexuality and identity, see Margaret Coulson's essay in *Homosexuality: Power and Politics*, and the articles by Wendy Clark and Deirdre English *et. al* in *Feminist Review*, No 11, 1982.

Chapter 3

The traditional concept of socialism to which we refer is drawn from the *Communist Manifesto*, Marx's *Critique of the Gotha Programme*, and Engels's *Anti-Duhring*. On the incompatibility of socialism and the family and the effects of the family system in society we are indebted to Michele Barrett and Mary McIntosh's *The Antisocial Family* (London: Verso, 1982) though we differ from their analysis of the strength of the family in contemporary society and their political perspectives. The quotation on page 73 is from Marx's *The Civil War in France*, 1870.

Chapter 4

Trotsky's *The Revolution Betrayed* is still, for all its age, the best overall account of the dynamics of Soviet society and is equally applicable to many of the newer 'communist' countries. A current edition is that of Pathfinder Press, New York, 1973. Information on the position of gay people in communist countries is scattered in various books and articles; on Cuba it is assembled in Allen Young's *Gays Under the Cuban Revolution* (San Francisco: Gay Sunshine Press, 1982).

On the position of women, Tamara Volkova's *Women and Russia* (London: Sheba, 1982) the *Labour Focus on Eastern*

Europe special issue on women and sexual politics, 1978, Hilda Scott's *Women & Socialism* (London: Allison & Busby, 1976) on Czechoslovakia and Katie Curtin's *Women in China* (New York: Pathfinder Press, 1975) provide useful information; *Women and the Cuban Revolution* edited by B. Stone (New York: Pathfinder Press, 1981) gives the official Cuban view.

Chapter 5

Many of the books referred to in relation to Chapter 1 contain discussion of objectives and strategy. Anne Phillips's *Hidden Hands* (London: Pluto, 1983) discusses the relevance of feminism to hours and wage issues; a more radical, though narrower, view of these issues is taken up in Kate Marshall's *Real Freedom* (London: Junius, 1982). We have drawn particularly heavily on the objectives outlined in the Fourth International Resolution, *Socialist Revolution and the Struggle for Women's Liberation*, adopted in 1979, printed in *Documents of the XI World Congress of the Fourth International* (New York: Intercontinental Press /Inprecor, 1980); and on the overall strategy of the *Transitional Programme for Socialist Revolution*, written by Trotsky and adopted by the Fourth International in 1938. (The best edition is that of Pathfinder Press, New York, 1973, which contains discussion elaborating the strategy of the programme).

On children's and young people's sexuality, see *Breaking the Silence*, edited by M. Burbridge and J. Walters (London: Joint Council for Gay Teenagers, 1981), and the articles edited by Daniel Tsang in *The Age Taboo* (London: Gay Men's Press, 1981).

There is some discussion of the political situation faced by gay people and how to deal with it in *Homosexuality: Power and Politics*, edited by The Gay Left Collective (London: Allison & Busby, 1980) and some sharp illustrations in Peter Tatchell's *The Battle for Bermondsey* (London: Heretic, 1983). The Labour Campaign for Gay Rights have published speeches from a fringe meeting at the 1982 Labour Party Conference in a special issue of their magazine *Gay Socialist*.